D1557919

Praise for Thanksgiving Delights

A Collection of Thanksgiving Recipes
Cookbook Delights Holiday Series Book 11

…"*Thanksgiving Delights* is more than a cookbook. Filled with fun facts, hundreds of recipes, and pleasant poetry, it's more like discovering a holiday treasure chest! The recipes are enticingly simple, yet elegant to serve. This cookbook is STUFFED with practical ideas for scrumptious food that you'll want to share!

Thanksgiving Delights is sure to become a family favorite for those who appreciate the value of holiday tradition and lasting memories. No serious cookbook collectors should be without this latest addition to the **Cookbook Delights Series!**"…

Kimberly Carter
Publicist

…"Discover some of the humble origins of the **Thanksgiving** traditions celebrated in the past and present in **Thanksgiving Delights Cookbook**. This spectacularly well-written and newest addition to the *Delights Cookbook Series* family has over 230 recipes and copious information pages and tidbits on history, folklore, and cultivation and gardening. In addition to scrumptious turkey and traditional side dishes, you will find inspiring poetry, nutritional information, and a useful and quick- reference index to help you find your favorite recipes easily. *Thanksgiving Delights* will soon be irreplaceable and treasured as a family heirloom."…

Mary Scripture-Smith
Graphic Designer

Praise for Thanksgiving Delights

A Collection of Thanksgiving Recipes
Cookbook Delights Holiday Series Book 11

…"*Thanksgiving Delights* is not only a cookbook, but a wealth of information about Thanksgiving. It includes fascinating facts, folklore, and the history of Thanksgiving, along with information on the symbols of Thanksgiving and poetry with Thanksgiving themes. It even includes information on how to grow cranberries, pumpkins, and sweet potatoes, which are staples of many Thanksgiving meals.

In addition to all of this information, it has a collection of over 230 delicious recipes that will be enjoyed by your family and friends.

This is a great value for the price and makes a wonderful gift."…

Dr. James G. Hood
Editor

Thanksgiving Delights

A Collection of Thanksgiving Recipes
Cookbook Delights Holiday Series Book 11

Karen Jean Matsko Hood

Current and Future Cookbooks

By Karen Jean Matsko Hood

Huckleberry Delights
Jalapeño Delights
Jerusalem Artichoke Delights
Jicama Delights
Kale Delights
Kiwi Delights
Kohlrabi Delights
Lavender Delights
Leek Delights
Lemon Delights
Lentil Delights
Lettuce Delights
Lime Delights
Lingonberry Delights
Lobster Delights
Loganberry Delights
Macadamia Nut Delights
Mango Delights
Marionberry Delights
Milk Delights
Mint Delights
Miso Delights
Mushroom Delights
Mussel Delights
Nectarine Delights
Oatmeal Delights
Olive Delights
Onion Delights
Orange Delights
Oregon Berry Delights
Oyster Delights
Papaya Delights
Parsley Delights
Parsnip Delights
Pea Delights
Peach Delights
Peanut Delights
Pear Delights
Pecan Delights
Pepper Delights
Persimmon Delights
Pine Nut Delights
Pineapple Delights
Pistachio Delights

Plum Delights
Pomegranate Delights
Pomelo Delights
Popcorn Delights
Poppy Seed Delights
Pork Delights
Potato Delights
Prickly Pear Cactus Delights
Prune Delights
Pumpkin Delights
Quince Delights
Quinoa Delights
Radish Delights
Raisin Delights
Raspberry Delights
Rhubarb Delights
Rice Delights
Rose Delights
Rosemary Delights
Rutabaga Delights
Salmon Delights
Salmonberry Delights
Salsify Delights
Savory Delights
Scallop Delights
Seaweed Delights
Serviceberry Delights
Sesame Delights
Shallot Delights
Shrimp Delights
Soybean Delights
Spinach Delights
Squash Delights
Star Fruit Delights
Strawberry Delights
Sunflower Seed Delights
Sweet Potato Delights
Swiss Chard Delights
Tangerine Delights
Tapioca Delights
Tayberry Delights
Tea Delights
Teaberry Delights
Thimbleberry Delights

Tofu Delights
Tomatillo Delights
Tomato Delights
Trout Delights
Truffle Delights
Tuna Delights
Turkey Delights
Turmeric Delights
Turnip Delights
Vanilla Delights
Walnut Delights
Wasabi Delights
Watermelon Delights
Wheat Delights
Wild Rice Delights
Yam Delights
Yogurt Delights
Zucchini Delights

CITY DELIGHTS

Chicago Delights
Coeur d'Alene Delights
Great Falls Delights
Honolulu Delights
Minneapolis Delights
Phoenix Delights
Portland Delights
Sandpoint Delights
Scottsdale Delights
Seattle Delights
Spokane Delights
St. Cloud Delights

FOSTER CARE

Foster Children Cookbook
   and Activity Book
Foster Children's Favorite
   Recipes
Holiday Cookbook for
   Foster Families

**GENERAL THEME
   DELIGHTS**

Appetizer Delights
Baby Food Delights
Barbeque Delights

Beer-Making Delights
Beverage Delights
Biscotti Delights
Bisque Delights
Blender Delights
Bread Delights
Bread Maker Delights
Breakfast Delights
Brunch Delights
Cake Delights
Campfire Food Delights
Candy Delights
Canned Food Delights
Cast Iron Delights
Cheesecake Delights
Chili Delights
Chowder Delights
Cocktail Delights
College Cooking Delights
Comfort Food Delights
Cookie Delights
Cooking for One Delights
Cooking for Two Delights
Cracker Delights
Crepe Delights
Crockpot Delights
Dairy Delights
Dehydrated Food Delights
Dessert Delights
Dinner Delights
Dutch Oven Delights
Foil Delights
Fondue Delights
Food Processor Delights
Fried Food Delights
Frozen Food Delights
Fruit Delights
Gelatin Delights
Grilled Delights
Hiking Food Delights
Ice Cream Delights
Juice Delights
Kid's Delights
Kosher Diet Delights

Liqueur-Making Delights
Liqueurs and Spirits Delights
Lunch Delights
Marinade Delights
Microwave Delights
Milk Shake and Malt Delights
Panini Delights
Pasta Delights
Pesto Delights
Phyllo Delights
Pickled Food Delights
Picnic Food Delights
Pizza Delights
Preserved Delights
Pudding and Custard Delights
Quiche Delights
Quick Mix Delights
Rainbow Delights
Salad Delights
Salsa Delights
Sandwich Delights
Sea Vegetable Delights
Seafood Delights
Smoothie Delights
Snack Delights
Soup Delights
Supper Delights
Tart Delights
Torte Delights
Tropical Delights
Vegan Delights
Vegetable Delights
Vegetarian Delights
Vinegar Delights
Wildflower Delights
Wine Delights
Winemaking Delights
Wok Delights

GIFTS-IN-A-JAR SERIES
Beverage Gifts-in-a-Jar
Christmas Gifts-in-a-Jar
Cookie Gifts-in-a-Jar
Gifts-in-a-Jar
Gifts-in-a-Jar Catholic

Gifts-in-a-Jar Christian
Holiday Gifts-in-a-Jar
Soup Gifts-in-a-Jar

HEALTH-RELATED DELIGHTS
Achalasia Diet Delights
Adrenal Health Diet Delights
Anti-Acid Reflux Diet
    Delights
Anti-Cancer Diet Delights
Anti-Inflammation Diet
    Delights
Anti-Stress Diet Delights
Arthritis Delights
Bone Health Diet Delights
Diabetic Diet Delights
Diet for Pink Delights
Fibromyalgia Diet Delights
Gluten-Free Diet Delights
Healthy Breath Diet Delights
Healthy Digestion Diet
    Delights
Healthy Heart Diet Delights
Healthy Skin Diet Delights
Healthy Teeth Diet Delights
High-Fiber Diet Delights
High-Iodine Diet Delights
High-Protein Diet Delights
Immune Health Diet Delights
Kidney Health Diet Delights
Lactose-Free Diet Delights
Liquid Diet Delights
Liver Health Diet Delights
Low-Calorie Diet Delights
Low-Carb Diet Delights
Low-Fat Diet Delights
Low-Sodium Diet Delights
Low-Sugar Diet Delights
Lymphoma Health Support
    Diet Delights
Multiple Sclerosis Healthy
    Diet Delights
No Flour No Sugar Diet
    Delights

Organic Food Delights
pH-Friendly Diet Delights
Pregnancy Diet Delights
Raw Food Diet Delights
Sjögren's Syndrome Diet
   Delights
Soft Food Diet Delights
Thyroid Health Diet Delights

HOLIDAY DELIGHTS

Christmas Delights, Vol. I-II
Easter Delights
Father's Day Delights
Fourth of July Delights
Grandparent's Day Delights
Halloween Delights
Hanukkah Delights
Labor Day Weekend Delights
Memorial Day Weekend
   Delights
Mother's Day Delights
New Year's Delights
St. Patrick's Day Delights
Thanksgiving Delights
Valentine Delights

HOOD AND MATSKO
FAMILY FAVORITES

Hood and Matsko Family
   Appetizers Cookbook
Hood and Matsko Family
   Beverages Cookbook
Hood and Matsko Family
   Breads and Rolls
   Cookbook
Hood and Matsko Family
   Breakfasts Cookbook
Hood and Matsko Family
   Cakes Cookbook
Hood and Matsko Family
   Candies Cookbook
Hood and Matsko Family
   Casseroles Cookbook
Hood and Matsko Family
   Cookies Cookbook
Hood and Matsko Family

Desserts Cookbook
Hood and Matsko Family
   Dressings, Sauces, and
   Condiments Cookbook
Hood and Matsko Family
   Ethnic Cookbook
Hood and Matsko Family
   Jams, Jellies, Syrups,
   Preserves, and Conserves
Hood and Matsko Family
   Main Dishes Cookbook
Hood and Matsko Family,
   Pies Cookbook
Hood and Matsko Family
   Preserving Cookbook
Hood and Matsko Family
   Salads and Salad Dressings
Hood and Matsko Family
   Side Dishes Cookbook
Hood and Matsko Family
   Vegetable Cookbook
Hood and Matsko Family,
   Aunt Katherine's Recipe
   Collection, Vol. I-II
Hood and Matsko Family,
   Grandma Bert's Recipe
   Collection, Vol. I-IV

HOOD AND MATSKO
FAMILY HOLIDAY

Hood and Matsko Family
   Favorite Birthday Recipes
Hood and Matsko Family
   Favorite Christmas Recipes
Hood and Matsko Family
   Favorite Christmas Sweets
Hood and Matsko Family
   Easter Cookbook
Hood and Matsko Family
   Favorite Thanksgiving
   Recipes

INTERNATIONAL
DELIGHTS

African Delights
African American Delights

Australian Delights
Austrian Delights
Brazilian Delights
Canadian Delights
Chilean Delights
Chinese Delights
Czechoslovakian Delights
English Delights
Ethiopian Delights
Fijian Delights
French Delights
German Delights
Greek Delights
Hungarian Delights
Icelandic Delights
Indian Delights
Irish Delights
Italian Delights
Korean Delights
Mexican Delights
Native American Delights
Polish Delights
Russian Delights
Scottish Delights
Slovenian Delights
Swedish Delights
Thai Delights
The Netherlands Delights
Yugoslavian Delights
Zambian Delights

REGIONAL DELIGHTS

Glacier National Park
   Delights
Northwest Regional Delights
Oregon Coast Delights
Schweitzer Mountain Delights
Southwest Regional Delights
Tropical Delights
Washington Wine Country
   Delights
Wine Delights of Walla
   Walla Wineries
Yellowstone National Park
   Delights

SEASONAL DELIGHTS

Autumn Harvest Delights
Spring Harvest Delights
Summer Harvest Delights
Winter Harvest Delights

SPECIAL EVENTS DELIGHTS

Birthday Delights
Coffee Klatch Delights
Super Bowl Delights
Tea Time Delights

STATE DELIGHTS

Alaska Delights
Arizona Delights
Georgia Delights
Hawaii Delights
Idaho Delights
Illinois Delights
Iowa Delights
Louisiana Delights
Minnesota Delights
Montana Delights
North Dakota Delights
Oregon Delights
South Dakota Delights
Texas Delights
Washington Delights

U.S. TERRITORIES DELIGHTS

Cruzan Delights
U.S. Virgin Island Delights

MISCELLANEOUS COOKBOOKS

Getaway Studio Cookbook
The Soup Doctor's Cookbook

BILINGUAL DELIGHTS SERIES

Apple Delights, English-
   French Edition
Apple Delights, English-
   Russian Edition
Apple Delights, English-
   Spanish Edition

Huckleberry Delights,
English-French Edition
Huckleberry Delights,
English-Russian Edition
Huckleberry Delights,
English-Spanish Edition
CATHOLIC DELIGHTS SERIES
Apple Delights Catholic
Coffee Delights Catholic
Easter Delights Catholic
Huckleberry Delights
Catholic
Tea Delights Catholic
CATHOLIC BILINGUAL DELIGHTS SERIES
Apple Delights Catholic,
English-French Edition
Apple Delights Catholic,
English-Russian Edition
Apple Delights Catholic,
English-Spanish Edition
Huckleberry Delights
Catholic, English-Spanish
Edition

CHRISTIAN DELIGHTS SERIES
Apple Delights Christian
Coffee Delights Christian
Easter Delights Christian
Huckleberry Delights
Christian
Tea Delights Christian
CHRISTIAN BILINGUAL DELIGHTS SERIES
Apple Delights Christian,
English-French Edition
Apple Delights Christian,
English-Russian Edition
Apple Delights Christian,
English-Spanish Edition
Huckleberry Delights
Christian, English-Spanish
Edition
FUNDRAISING COOKBOOKS
Ask about our fundraising
cookbooks to help raise
funds for your
organization.

The above books are also available in bilingual versions. Please contact Whispering Pine Press International, Inc., for details.

Please note that some books are future books and are currently in production. Please contact us for availability date. Prices are subject to change without notice.

The above list of books is not all-inclusive. For a complete list please visit our website or contact us at:

Whispering Pine Press International, Inc.
Your Northwest Book Publishing Company
P.O. Box 214
Spokane Valley, WA 99037-0214 USA
Phone: (509) 928-8700 | Fax: (509) 922-9949
Email: sales@whisperingpinepress.com
Publisher Websites: www.WhisperingPinePress.com
www.WhisperingPinePressBookstore.com
Blog: www.WhisperingPinePressBlog.com

Thanksgiving Delights

A Collection of Thanksgiving Recipes
Cookbook Delights Holiday Series Book 11

Karen Jean Matsko Hood

Published by:

Whispering Pine Press International, Inc.
Your Northwest Book Publishing Company
P.O. Box 214
Spokane Valley, WA 99037-0214 USA
Phone: (509) 928-8700 | Fax: (509) 922-9949
Email: sales@whisperingpinepress.com
Publisher Websites: www.WhisperingPinePress.com
www.WhisperingPinePressBookstore.com
Blog: www.WhisperingPinePressBlog.com
SAN 253-200X
Printed in the U.S.A.
Published by Whispering Pine Press International, Inc.

P.O. Box 214
Spokane Valley, Washington 99037-0214 USA

For sales outside the United States, please contact the Whispering
Pine Press International, Inc., International Sales Department.

Book and Cover Design by Artistic Design Service
P.O. Box 1782
Spokane Valley, WA 99037-1782 USA
www.ArtisticDesignService.com

Library of Congress Number (LCCN): 2014 pending

Hood, Karen Jean Matsko
    Title: Thanksgiving Delights Cookbook: A Collection of
Thanksgiving Recipes: Cookbook Delights Holiday
Series Book 11

    p.   cm.

ISBN: 978-1-59434-164-9   case bound
ISBN: 978-1-59434-165-6   perfect bound
ISBN: 978-1-59434-166-3   spiral bound
ISBN: 978-1-59434-167-0   comb bound
ISBN: 978-1-59434-170-0   E-PDF
ISBN: 978-1-59210-475-8   E-PUB
ISBN: 978-1-59434-863-1   E-PRC

First Edition: January 2014

1. Cookery (*Thanksgiving Delights Cookbook: A Collection of
Thanksgiving Recipes: Cookbook Delights Holiday Series
Book 11*)   1. Title

Thanksgiving Delights Cookbook

A Collection of Thanksgiving Recipes
Cookbook Delights Holiday Series Book 11

Gift Inscription

To: _____

From: _____

Date: _____

Special Message: _____

_____

_____

_____

_____

_____

_____

_____

*It is always nice to receive a personal note to
create a special memory.*

www.ThanksgivingDelights.com
www.WhisperingPinePress.com
www.WhisperingPinePressBookstore.com

Dedications

To my husband and best friend, Jim.

To our seventeen children: Gabriel, Brianne Kristina and her husband Moulik Vinodkumar Kothari, Marissa Kimberly and her husband Kevin Matthew Franck, Janelle Karina and her husband Paul Joseph Turcotte, Mikayla Karlene, Kyler James, Kelsey Katrina, Corbin Joel, Caleb Jerome, Keisha Kalani Hiwot, Devontay Joshua, Kianna Karielle Selam, Rosy Kiara, Mercedes Katherine, Jasmine Khalia Wengel, Cheyenne Krystal, and Annalise Kaylee Marie.

To our grandchildren and foster grandchildren: Courtney, Lorenzo, and Leah.

To my brother, Stephen, and his wife, Karen.

To my husband's ten siblings: Gary, Colleen, John, Dan, Mary, Ray, Ann, Teresa, Barbara, Agnes, and their families.

In loving memory of my mom, who passed away in 2007; my dad, who passed away in 1976; and my sister, Sandy, who passed away due to multiple sclerosis in 1999.

To Sandy's three sons: Monte, Bradley, and Derek. To Monte's wife, Sarah, and their children: Liam, Alice, Charlie, and Samuel and their foster children. To Bradley's wife, Shawnda, and their children: Anton, Isaac, and Isabel.

To our foster children past and present: Krystal, Sara, Rebecca, Janice, Devontay Joshua, Mercedes Katherine, Zha'Nell, Makia, Onna, Cheyenne Krystal, Onna Marie, Nevaeh, and Zada, our future foster children, and all foster children everywhere.

To the Court Appointed Special Advocate (CASA) Volunteer Program in the judicial system which benefits abused and neglected children.

To the Literacy Campaign dedicated to promoting literacy throughout the world.

Acknowledgements

The author would like to acknowledge all those individuals who helped me during my time in writing this book. Appreciation is extended for all their support and effort they put into this project.

Deep gratitude and profound thanks are owed to my husband, Jim, for giving freely of his time and encouragement during this project. Also, thanks are owed to my children Gabriel, Brianne Kristina and her husband Moulik Vinodkumar Kothari, Marissa Kimberly and her husband Kevin Matthew Franck, Janelle Karina and her husband Paul Joseph Turcotte, Mikayla Karlene, Kyler James, Kelsey Katrina, Corbin Joel, Caleb Jerome, Keisha Kalani Hiwot, Devontay Joshua, Kianna Karielle Selam, Rosy Kiara, Mercedes Katherine, Jasmine Khalia Wengel, Cheyenne Krystal, and Annalise Kaylee Marie. All of these persons inspire my writing.

Thanks are due to Beverly Koerperich and Sharron Thompson for their assistance in editing and typing this manuscript for publication. Thanks go to Artistic Design Service for their assistance in formatting and providing a graphic design of this manuscript for publication. This project could not have been completed without them.

Many thanks are due to members of my family, all of whom were very supportive during the time it took to complete this project. Their patience and support are greatly appreciated.

xviii

Thanksgiving Delights Cookbook

Table of Contents

Thanksgiving Delights Cookbook

A Collection of Thanksgiving Recipes
Cookbook Delights Holiday Series Book 11

Introduction

Thanksgiving is such a wonderful time of year! Family and friends gather together to share food and recipes in the spirit of community sharing. I hope you will enjoy this collection of Thanksgiving recipes for the holiday and throughout the year.

Thanksgiving has an interesting history of facts and folklore. Some of this Thanksgiving folklore is included in this book. As a poet, I found it enjoyable to color this cookbook with poetry so that readers could savor the metaphorical richness of Thanksgiving as well as its literal flavor. Also included in this *Thanksgiving Delights Cookbook* are some articles on history, cultivation, and botanical information, along with interesting facts about Thanksgiving

The *Cookbook Delights Series* would not be complete without *Thanksgiving Delights* because we want to include this holiday of giving thanks. We hope you enjoy reading it as well as trying out all the recipes. This cookbook is designed for easy use and is organized into alphabetical sections: appetizers and dips; beverages; breads and rolls; breakfasts; cakes; candies; cookies; desserts; dressings, sauces, and condiments; jams, jellies, and syrups; main dishes; pies; preserving; salads; side dishes; soups; and wines and spirits.

Do enjoy reading about Thanksgiving, but most importantly, have fun with those you care about while you are cooking.

Following is a collection of recipes gathered and modified to bring you *Thanksgiving Delights Cookbook: A Collection of Thanksgiving Recipes, Cookbook Delights Series* by Karen Jean Matsko Hood.

Thanksgiving Delights Cookbook

A Collection of Thanksgiving Recipes
Cookbook Delights Holiday Series Book 11

Thanksgiving
Botanical Classification

Thanksgiving Botanical Classification

Scientific Name	Common Name	Main Features
Vaccinium macrocarpon	Cranberry (commercially grown variety)	Low growing, trailing, sprawling habit; evergreen leaves are simple and alternate, light green and maroon colored when young, shiny and dark green when mature; flowers light pink, grow in clusters of 4 or 5; fruit is red berry.
Cucurbitaceae moschata	Kentucky field or cheese group of pumpkins; Butternut squash	Stem hard, smoothly grooved; leaf nearly round to moderately lobed, soft; skin tan color (widely used for commercially canned pumpkin); seeds white to brown, often plump and surface sometimes split or wrinkled.
C. pepo	Jack-o'-lantern group, small sugar and miniature pumpkins; Acorn and Vegetable Spaghetti squash	Stem hard, angular, grooved, and prickly; leaf palmately lobed, often deeply cut, prickly; seed dull white to tan, smooth.
C. argyrosperma (C. mixta)	Cushaws and related types of pumpkin	Stem hard, angular, grooved; leaf moderately lobed, soft; seeds white, may be large, surface smooth or split.
Ipomoea batatas	Sweet Potato	Tuberous-rooted perennial of morning glory family, usually grown as an annual; stems form running vine, usually prostrate and slender, with milky juice; leaves ovate-cordate, palmately veined, angular or lobed, green or purplish; flowers pale violet or white; fruits are pods with 1 to 4 seeds per pod, flattened, hard-coated, angular.

Thanksgiving Delights Cookbook

A Collection of Thanksgiving Recipes
Cookbook Delights Holiday Series Book 11

Thanksgiving Cultivation and Gardening

Thanksgiving Cultivation and Gardening

Cranberries: Contrary to popular belief, cranberries do not need a bog, or even soggy soil, to thrive. In the wild, they are found near water, but they do not grow in it. Cranberry bogs in America, where cranberries are commercially grown, are deliberately flooded to make harvesting easier. After the berries are harvested, the bogs are drained again.

Cranberries can be grown almost anywhere in your garden where the soil is acidic. Poor, sandy, or peaty soils suit them best. They will grow in most non-alkaline soils and like some peat and/or rotted bark to root into. Cranberries can be planted to act as ground cover in a shrub border where azaleas, rhododendrons, and heathers thrive. They can also be grown among blueberry bushes. If your soil is not sufficiently acidic (pH 6.2 or below), cranberries can be grown in containers of all shapes and sizes.

Never use manure or any animal-based fertilizer on blueberries or cranberries, because the roots are easily killed by chemical scorching. Plant cranberries 12 inches apart. They will fill the space between them in a couple of years.

If growing cranberries in a container, use ericaceous compost. Two-year-old plants may give an occasional berry the first summer after planting but should really start setting on the following year.

If growing cranberries in a hanging basket, watch out for the critical period in September and early October when it is easy to relax and pay less attention to watering. This is the time when next year's flower buds will have formed, unseen, and they can be damaged or even aborted by lack of water.

Cranberries need very little feeding. In fact, they are easily killed by too much fertilizer, especially that used to feed tomatoes and other fruits and vegetables. A small pinch of ericaceous fertilizer given in April/May and again in August keeps the plants active until autumn. They have a huge growth spurt in mid-summer after flowering in June.

Birds and other pests which usually flock to fruit crops leave cranberries alone. Plant failure is usually due to lack of attention to watering or over feeding.

Pumpkins and Winter Squash: Pumpkins and winter squash are very tender vegetables. Thus, they should not be planted until all danger of frost is past and the soil has thoroughly warmed. Plant from late May in northern locations to early July in extremely southern areas.

Vining pumpkins and squash require a minimum of 50 to 100 square feet per hill. Plant seeds 1 inch deep (4 or 5 seeds per hill). Allow 5 to 6 feet between hills, spaced in rows 10 to 15 feet apart. When the young plants are well established, thin each hill to the best 2 or 3 plants.

Plant semi-bush varieties 1 inch deep (4 to 5 seeds per hill) and thin to the best 2 plants per hill. Allow 4 feet between hills and 8 feet between rows.

Plant miniature varieties 1 inch deep with 2 or 3 seeds every 2 feet in a row. Rows should be 6 to 8 feet apart, with seedlings thinned to the best plant every 2 feet when they have their first true leaves.

Plant bush varieties 1 inch deep (1 or 2 seeds per foot of row) and thin to a single plant every 3 feet. Allow 4 to 6 feet between rows.

Plants should be kept free from weeds by hoeing and shallow cultivation. Irrigate if an extended dry period occurs in early summer. Pumpkins and winter squash tolerate short periods of hot, dry weather fairly well.

Bees are necessary for pollination and may be killed by insecticides. When insecticides are used, they should be applied only in late afternoon or early evening when the blossoms have closed for the day and bees are no longer visiting the blossoms.

Pumpkins and winter squash can be harvested whenever they are a deep, solid color and the rind is hard. If vines remain healthy, harvest in late September or early October, before heavy frosts. Cut fruit from the vines carefully, using pruning shears or a sharp knife, and leave 3 to 4 inches of stem attached. Snapping the stems from the vines results in many broken or missing "handles." Pumpkins and squash without stems do not keep well. Wear gloves when harvesting fruit because many varieties have sharp prickles on their stems. Avoid cutting and bruising pumpkins and squash when handling them. Fruits that are not fully mature or that have been injured or subjected to heavy frost do not keep.

After picking, cure pumpkins and winter squash. (Note: Acorn squash is an exception. They like lower temperatures than other squash and should not be cured. Keep them at 45 to 50 degrees F., not over 55 degrees, or they will turn stringy and dry.) Spread squash and pumpkins on the grass or on an open porch where the sun can reach them. Protect from frost. If weather is rainy, cure inside at 70 to 80 degrees F. Cure for 10 to 14 days before storing. Store at 55 to 60 degrees F. with 60 to 70 percent humidity, in a single layer, an inch or so apart.

Common problems in growing pumpkins and winter squash include powdery mildew and insect infestation. Powdery mildew causes a white, powdery mold growth on the upper surfaces of the leaves. The growth can kill the leaves prematurely and interfere with proper ripening.

Cucumber beetles and squash bugs attack seedlings, vines, and both immature and mature fruits. Be alert for an infestation of cucumber beetles and squash bugs, as populations build in late summer. These insects can damage the mature fruits, marring their appearance and making them less likely to keep properly.

Sweet Potatoes: Sweet potatoes are started from plants called "slips." Transplant slips as soon as soil warms up after the last frost. Always buy plants grown from certified disease-free roots. To grow your own slips, place several sweet potato roots about 1 inch apart in a hotbed and cover with 2 inches of sand or light soil. Add another 1 inch of sand when shoots begin to appear. Keep the soil moist throughout the sprouting period, but do not let it become waterlogged. Keep soil temperature between 70 and 80 degrees F. Plants are ready to pull in about 6 weeks, when they are rooted and 6 to 8 inches tall.

Set plants 12 to 18 inches apart, preferably on a wide, raised ridge about 8 inches high. Allow at least 3 to 4 feet between rows.

After early cultivation, sweet potatoes need minimum care to keep down weeds. Irrigate if an extended drought occurs. Do not water during the last 3 to 4 weeks before harvest to protect the developing roots.

Dig your crop around the time of the first frost in the fall. Use a spading fork or shovel, being careful to not bruise or cut the roots. In case of frost, cut the vines from the roots immediately to prevent decay spreading from the vines to the roots, and dig the sweet potatoes as soon as possible.

Ideally, roots should be allowed to dry on the ground for 2 to 3 hours, then placed in a warm room for curing (85 degrees F. and 85 percent humidity) for 10 to 14 days. After curing, store at 55 degrees F. Sweet potatoes should be handled as little as possible to avoid scuffing and bruising.

To prevent diseases, plant varieties with multiple resistance, use certified plants, and rotate their location in the garden.

Thanksgiving Delights Cookbook

A Collection of Thanksgiving Recipes
Cookbook Delights Holiday Series Book 11

Thanksgiving Facts

Thanksgiving Facts

The first recorded Thanksgiving observance was held in Charleston, Massachusetts, on June 29, 1671, by proclamation of the town's governing council.

President George Washington made the first national proclamation of Thanksgiving on October 3, 1789, creating the first Thanksgiving Day designated by the national government of the United States and recommending Thursday, November 26, of that year the day it was to be observed.

In the United States, certain kinds of food are traditionally served at Thanksgiving meals. The centrally featured item is the turkey. Other dishes associated with the Thanksgiving meal are stuffing, mashed potatoes and gravy, sweet potatoes, cranberry sauce, corn, and pumpkin pie.

Even though the turkey is now the central part of the Thanksgiving meal, that was not always so. Before the 20th century, pork ribs were the most commonly consumed food on the holiday since the animals were usually slaughtered in November. Turkeys were once so abundant in the wild that they were eaten throughout the year and were considered commonplace, with pork ribs rarely being available except during the holiday season. The turkey has also displaced, for the most part, the traditional Christmas roast goose or beef of Britain and Europe.

In New York City, the Macy's Thanksgiving Day Parade is held annually every Thanksgiving Day. The parade features floats with specific themes, scenes from Broadway plays, large balloons of cartoon characters and television personalities, and high school marching bands. The float that traditionally ends the Macy's Parade is the Santa Claus float. This float is a sign that the Christmas season has begun. Thanksgiving parades also occur in many cities such as Plymouth, Houston, Philadelphia (which claims the oldest parade), and Detroit (where it is the only major parade of the year).

Thanksgiving Delights Cookbook

A Collection of Thanksgiving Recipes
Cookbook Delights Holiday Series Book 11

Thanksgiving Folklore

Thanksgiving Folklore

The traditional story of the first Thanksgiving tells us about Squanto teaching the pilgrims in Massachusetts how to cultivate corn and grow native vegetables. After a successful harvest, they celebrated and invited the Native Americans to join them.

According to legend, Ben Franklin thought the North American wild turkey should be the national bird. Of course, the turkey of his day was nothing like the domesticated descendants we know today. The wild turkey of Ben Franklin's day was a brightly plumed, cunning bird of flight. But the turkey lost—at least temporarily. The turkey, as a symbol, slipped into oblivion for decades before finding a new niche in American life.

Thanksgiving had been a local holiday in some places in New England. Two centuries later, during the Civil War, Abraham Lincoln, looking for ways to bring the nation together, declared Thanksgiving a national holiday. And, with it, the turkey regained respect and visibility.

The timing of Thanksgiving—at the point in the fall season when the traditional harvesting is completed—also contributes to its symbolic power. The holiday is the beneficiary of all the symbolism of the various kinds of harvest feasts that were celebrated all over the old World, Europe, and Africa. This includes gourds, squashes, and all kinds of autumnal things.

Although the turkey is central, it is surrounded by as many dishes as possible. The success of the meal is not only in terms of how much people eat, but also in terms of how many different dishes are offered at that meal. Even as the turkey is "all-American," other dishes can be as diverse as the population itself: from pasta to sweet-potato latkes to collard, mustard, and turnip greens. Each ethnic group adds its particular flavor to the meal.

The idea of the Thanksgiving feast is to eat more than you can possibly eat. You have to eat until you are groaning. The whole thing is about stuffing, overeating, abundance, cornucopia. The turkey is not the only thing being stuffed.

In this day and age, Thanksgiving Day is not only a day of feasting and family but of parades, races, and last, but not least, football.

Thanksgiving Delights Cookbook

A Collection of Thanksgiving Recipes
Cookbook Delights Holiday Series Book 11

Thanksgiving History

Thanksgiving History

The story of Thanksgiving is basically the story of the Pilgrims and their thankful community feast at Plymouth, Massachusetts. The Mayflower was a small ship crowded with men, women, and children, besides the sailors on board. Most of those making the trip on the Mayflower were non-Separatists but were hired to protect the company's interests. The rest of the group were originally members of the English Separatist Church (a Puritan sect). Their leadership came from a religious congregation who had fled a volatile political environment in the East Midlands of England for the relative calm of Holland in the Netherlands to preserve their religion. Concerned with losing their cultural identity, the group later arranged with English investors to establish a new colony in North America.

Initially the trip went smoothly, but underway they were met with strong winds and storms. One of these caused a main beam to crack, and although they were more than half the way to their destination, the possibility of turning back was considered. Using a "great iron screw" (probably a piece of house construction equipment) brought along by the colonists, they repaired the ship sufficiently to continue.

With the charter for the Plymouth Council for New England incomplete by the time the colonists departed England (it would be granted while they were in transit), on November 13, they arrived without a patent. Some of the passengers, aware of the situation, suggested that without a patent in place, they were free to do as they chose upon landing and ignore the contract with the investors. To address this issue, a brief contract, later to be known as the Mayflower Compact, was drafted promising cooperation among the settlers "for the general good of the Colony unto which we promise all due submission and obedience." It was ratified by majority rule, with 41 adult male passengers signing. At this time, John Carver was chosen as the colony's first governor. This merged group was called the "Pilgrims."

They were ill-equipped to face the winter in this new land, and it was a devastating one. During the winter most of the passengers remained on board the Mayflower, suffering an outbreak of a contagious disease described as a mixture of scurvy, pneumonia, and tuberculosis. When it ended, there were only 53 persons still alive, half of the passengers and half of the crew. Throughout the winter, some of the men worked on building houses, and on March 21, 1621, the surviving passengers left the Mayflower.

On March 16, 1621, the first formal contact with the Native Americans occurred. A Native American named Samoset, originally from Pemaquid Point in modern Maine, walked boldly into the midst of the settlement and proclaimed, "Welcome, Englishmen!" He had learned some English from fishermen who worked off the coast of Maine and gave them a brief introduction to the region's history and geography. It was during this meeting that the Pilgrims found out that the previous residents of the Native American village, Patuxet, had probably died of smallpox. They also discovered that the supreme leader of the region was a Wampanoag Native American *sachem* (chief) by the name of Massasoit; and they learned of the existence of Squanto (also known by his full Massachusett name of Tisquantum), a Native American originally from Patuxet. Squanto had spent time in Europe and spoke English quite well. Samoset spent the night in Plymouth and agreed to arrange a meeting with some of Massasoit's men.

With the help of a group of these local Native Americans who befriended them and taught them how to cultivate corn, grow native vegetables, and store them, the harvest of 1621 was a bountiful one. That winter passed by without much harm.

The autumn celebration in late 1621 that has become known as "The First Thanksgiving" was not known as such to the Pilgrims. The Pilgrims did recognize a celebration known as a "Thanksgiving," which was a solemn ceremony of praise and thanks to God for a congregation's good fortune. The first such Thanksgiving, as the Pilgrims would have called it, did not occur until 1623, in response to the good news of the arrival of additional colonists and supplies. That event probably occurred in July and consisted of a full day of prayer and worship and probably very little revelry.

It is not certain that turkey was a part of their feast. Governor William Bradford wrote of sending men out for wild ducks and geese. Native Americans also supplied venison. It is unlikely that first feast included pumpkin pie. Their supply of flour had been long diminished, so there was likely no bread or pastries of any kind. However, they did eat boiled pumpkin, and they produced a type of fried bread from their corn crop. There was no milk, cider, potatoes, or butter. There were no domestic cattle for dairy products, and the newly discovered potato was still considered by many Europeans to be poisonous. But, they did have fish, berries, watercress, lobster, dried fruit, clams, and plums.

Days of thanksgiving were celebrated throughout the colonies after fall harvests. All thirteen colonies did not, however, celebrate Thanksgiving at the same time until October 1777. George Washington was the first president to declare the holiday, in 1789.

By the mid-1800s many states observed a Thanksgiving holiday. Meanwhile, the poet and editor Sarah J. Hale had begun lobbying for a national Thanksgiving holiday. During the Civil War, President Abraham Lincoln, looking for ways to unite the nation, discussed the subject with Hale. In 1863 he gave his Thanksgiving Proclamation, declaring the last Thursday in November a day of thanksgiving.

Thanksgiving was proclaimed by every president after Lincoln. The date was changed a few times. In 1939, 1940, and 1941, the Great Depression era, Franklin D. Roosevelt, seeking to lengthen the Christmas shopping season, proclaimed Thanksgiving the third Thursday in November. Controversy followed and Congress passed a joint resolution in 1941 decreeing that Thanksgiving should fall on the fourth Thursday of November, where it remains today.

Thanksgiving Delights Cookbook

A Collection of Thanksgiving Recipes
Cookbook Delights Holiday Series Book 11

Thanksgiving Nutrition and Health

Thanksgiving Nutrition and Health

Cranberries: Fresh cranberries contain the highest levels of their beneficial nutrients. One-half cup of cranberries contains about 11 percent of the recommended daily value of vitamin C. Cranberries have long been valued for their ability to help prevent and treat urinary tract infections. Recent studies suggest they may also promote gastrointestinal and oral health, prevent the formation of kidney stones, lower LDL (bad) and raise HDL (good) cholesterol, aid in recovery from stroke, and even help prevent cancer.

Pumpkin and Winter Squash: The orange flesh of the pumpkin is a dead giveaway that it is a source of beta carotene, which is a powerful antioxidant. Beta carotene is converted to vitamin A in the body. Vitamin A is essential for healthy skin, vision, bone development, and many other functions.

Winter squash is also an excellent source of vitamin A. It is a very good source of vitamin C, potassium, dietary fiber, and manganese. In addition, winter squash is a good source of folate, omega-3 fatty acids, thiamin, vitamin B5, vitamin B6, niacin, and copper.

Sweet Potatoes: The sweet potato has been used as a food source since before recorded history. It is a nutritionally dense food and is loaded with vitamins, minerals, and nutrients. It is one of the single best sources of beta carotene (vitamin A) to be found in nature. Sweet potatoes are a good source of vitamins B6, C, and E, as well as calcium, potassium, thiamin, and iron. They are fiber-rich, low in sodium, and virtually fat free.

Turkey: The USDA recommends 2 or 3 servings of meat, fish, or poultry per day. A serving of any type of cooked meat is equal to 3 ounces and is about the size of a deck of cards. Compared with other meats, turkey has fewer calories, less fat, less cholesterol, and very little sodium, but it is high in protein, vitamins, and minerals.

Most of the fat in turkey is within the skin, and most of the fat within the meat is in the dark meat. The white meat with the skin removed is a good food source for people on low-fat and/or low sodium diets. The meat fiber is easier to digest than other types of meat, which makes it a good choice for individuals who may have digestive problems. Turkey is an excellent source of several important vitamins and nutrients such as iron, niacin, zinc, potassium, and B vitamins.

Thanksgiving Delights Cookbook

A Collection of Thanksgiving Recipes
Cookbook Delights Holiday Series Book 11

Poetry

A Collection of Poetry with Thanksgiving Themes

Table of Contents

Thankful Together

In faith, in prayer, this community
   can be thankful together.
Today we show appreciation for this holiday,
   Thanksgiving Day!

A new beginning we live today
   A day we thank each other
For this country, brave and free.
   Together we can work to find solutions.

We join hands to solve
   injustice and unfairness that may exist.
Yet if we join in love and laughter,
   the bouquet of fall flowers can remind us

To transform our faith and love.
   Sunset, crimson, yellow, gold.,
Colors of the sunset with shades of sunrise,
   land of our forefathers, future of our children.

Let us show thanks today
   and each day of the future.

Karen Jean Matsko Hood©2014
Published in *Thanksgiving Delights Cookbook*, 2014
By Whispering Pine Press International, Inc., 2014

Haikus of Thanksgiving

Burst layered sunrise
Autumn bouquet of colors
Thanksgiving sunrise.

Pilgrims gather gourds
Spit turns pork over hot fires
Hungry stomachs fill.

Let the fun begin
Children chatter 'round the bend
Autumn stars twinkle.

Open our eyes, see
Morn, noon, and night together
Pray the pilgrim prayer.

Karen Jean Matsko Hood©2014
Published in *Thanksgiving Delights Cookbook*, 2014
By Whispering Pine Press International, Inc., 2014

Indian Paintbrush

The paintbrush of the Aboriginal American
Jostles in the glacial breeze,
Before my eyes with awe,
Imbues legends of mystery and wonder,
Portraits of rose, rust, and burgundy,

Enlightenment for the ancient and young.
The tradition of the native brush strokes
Decipher the lacquer of the folklore
That sways in the wind.
Roots below the soul reach

Deep within the craggy burl.
Local bare and scraggly branches
Crumble to the universal call;
Intrinsic whispers shout.
Working honeybees stop and strain, to

Listen to the paintbrush,
Thankful for the deeper maxim,
Wisdom of the plant beard.
Finally, the mythos' secret is understood.
Honeybees do smile and wave

Back to their fellow creatures
They carry the tincture of wisdom,
And the wind does rest.

Karen Jean Matsko Hood ©2014
Published in *Thanksgiving Delights Cookbook*, 2014
By Whispering Pine Press International, Inc., 2014

Thank You!

Often we forget these two simple words.
Thank you.

We have so many blessings, so much bounty,
Great things we take for granted.
Freedom, love, and relationships,
Spring air, fresh breeze upon our face,
Night skies decorated with stars that twinkle,
Followed by morning rays that illuminate
petals of roses kissed with dew.
Thank you.

What about the elderly with lines carved in their face
like a road map with destinations unknown.
Do we forget their tireless war to make us free
and their wisdom of many years gone by?
Or do we let them sit in nursing homes
tucked away from sight,
so we do not have to clutter our landscape
with sights not attractive to our spoiled eyes?

Thank you for our gift of life.
We appreciate our glorious country;
peace from hardship
in the land of the brave and free.

Karen Jean Matsko Hood ©2014
Published in *Thanksgiving Delights Cookbook*, 2014
By Whispering Pine Press International, Inc., 2014

Autumn Snow

Why does autumn bring the snow
When summer drops the ice?
Waiting for the veins of henna,
Crimson maple leaves,
Odiferous moldy acorns
Provoke fuzzy gossamer
To package pungent aromas.
Spicy apple astringent,
Warm cider pressed, ever
Punctuated with the fragrance of
Pumpkin seeds roasting in the oven,
Cinnamon spice,
Vagabond leaves
Crunchy in the snow.

Karen Jean Matsko Hood ©2014
Published in *Thanksgiving Delights Cookbook*, 2014
By Whispering Pine Press International, Inc., 2014

Thankful for the Morning Sun

Thankful for the morning sun,
Thank you for the evening moon.
In between are clouds and kites
that rise above with muddy winds.
Oceans feed the rivers that run into the lakes
that lay still next to the skyward mountains.

Karen Jean Matsko Hood ©2014
Published in *Thanksgiving Delights Cookbook*, 2014
By Whispering Pine Press International, Inc., 2014

Moonlit Sun

How long will be my life?
I asked under the sunlit moon.
It seems I want to trade
My days of the magical
Worker bee with the giant
Sea turtle to bask in the
Hushful moonlit sun.

Karen Jean Matsko Hood ©2014
Published in *Thanksgiving Delights Cookbook*, 2014
By Whispering Pine Press International, Inc., 2014

Autumn Glow

Autumn appears. Ruddy glow shimmers
over crisp air. Pungent aroma
wears afternoon apparel,
noisy in the wind.

I am a basket of maple leaves
florid and crinkled with age,
scalloped from an artist's hand,
one far more powerful than words.

I snuggle with the oak leaves
much smaller than myself,
golden in color. I nestle with the acorns
strong and majestic, leathery and sullen.

I imbibe the heavy moist air
euphoric with nature, rolling in the sun
to watch over rotting pumpkin vines
blind-sided by the snap of weather.

Life's basket will give me rest,
while others may perish.
Dark tiny apple seeds and tough acorns
lay waiting, to germinate and
grow once more.

Karen Jean Matsko Hood ©2014
Published in *Thanksgiving Delights Cookbook*, 2014
By Whispering Pine Press International, Inc., 2014

Happy Thanksgiving

The air is cool, the season is fall.
Soon Thanksgiving will come to us all.
The turkeys are running for things to do.
In fact, a turkey brought this to you!

"Gobble Gobble" is a treasure from the Thanksgiving hour.
Just leave it up and watch its power.
In your house is where it works.
It cheers up those who stand and lurk.

These yummy treats are for your pleasure.
We've even included a little treasure.
Make two copies to give your friends.
They'll have warm fuzzies that never end.

We'll all have a smile upon our face.
No one will know who Gobble Gobbled this place.
Just one short day, your kindness to cast,
Or a big turkey will strike you fast.

And don't forget a nifty treat,
Like something cute or something sweet.
Please join the fun, let's really hear it.
And spread some Gobble Gobbles and Thanksgiving Spirit!

Directions:

- Enjoy treats!
- Leave the "GOBBLE GOBBLE" sign on your front door.
- Now you have 24 hours to copy this twice, draw two turkey shapes with "GOBBLE GOBBLE" written on them, and make up two treat bags.
- Deliver them to two neighbors who do not have a "GOBBLE GOBBLE" sign.
- Watch how far it goes!

Thanksgiving Delights Cookbook

A Collection of Thanksgiving Recipes
Cookbook Delights Holiday Series Book 11

Thanksgiving Symbols

Thanksgiving Symbols

Corn: Corn, or maize, was the first of the Indian Three Sisters. It is native to America. Corn came in many varieties—red, white, blue, and yellow. The Pilgrims had never seen it in England. It was new to their diet, but they might have starved without it.

Cornucopia: One of the most prominent Thanksgiving symbols, the cornucopia actually dates back to the ancient Greeks and Romans. The term (generally describing a horn-shaped basket filled with fruit, flowers, and other goodies) comes from the Latin *cornu copiae*, literally "horn of plenty." In Greek mythology, the cornucopia is a severed goat's horn, enchanted by Zeus to produce a never-ending supply of whatever the owner desires.

Cranberries: Cranberries grew wild in bogs along the New England coast. Squanto showed the Pilgrims where to find cranberries and how to dry them for the winter. As soon as the Pilgrims figured out how to sweeten the bitter little berries with maple sugar, they started making cranberry sauce. Cranberry sauce has been a turkey's favorite Thanksgiving partner every since.

Mayflower: Mayflower was the ship that carried the first Pilgrims to America in 1620. It was built around 1610 and probably had three masts and two decks. It probably measured about 90 feet long and weighed about 180 short tons (163 metric tons). Its master was Christopher Jones.

Native Americans: The area that would later become the Thirteen Colonies was also home to more than 500,000 Native Americans. Squanto, a Patuxet, is said to have taught the white settlers how to plant corn and fertilize it with dead fish. Massasoit of the Wampanoag helped the Pilgrims of Plymouth Colony.

Pilgrims: The early English settlers of New England became known as the Pilgrims. On September 16, 1620, forty-one Separatists and 61 other people from England became the first group of Pilgrims to journey to America.

Pumpkins: Pumpkins and squash together were the second of the Indian Three Sisters. The Pilgrims were introduced to the pumpkin by their Native American neighbors, and it has been a part of Thanksgiving ever since. Although we do not eat pumpkin very often anymore, the first Americans ate it all the time.

Thanksgiving: Thanksgiving itself is a symbolic representation of love, warmth, caring, and sharing.

Turkey: Turkey and Thanksgiving have gone together since before the beginning of the 20th century. No Thanksgiving feast is considered to be complete without a turkey as the main course.

Thanksgiving Delights Cookbook

A Collection of Thanksgiving Recipes
Cookbook Delights Holiday Series Book 11

RECIPES

Thanksgiving Delights Cookbook

A Collection of Thanksgiving Recipes
Cookbook Delights Holiday Series Book 11

Appetizers and Dips

Table of Contents

Did You Know? . . . .

Did you know that Plymouth Rock, the traditional site of disembarkation of William Bradford and the Mayflower Pilgrims, who founded Plymouth Colony, is described by some as "the most disappointing landmark in America" because of its small size and poor visitor access?

Cheese Cranberry Salsa Dip

This appetizer dip is a fresh combination of flavor to add to your holiday menu.

Ingredients:

    3   c. fresh cranberries, rinsed, drained
    ¼   c. minced green onions
    ½   c. sugar
    2   Tbs. fresh lemon juice
    2   Tbs. jalapeno peppers, minced, cored
    2   Tbs. fresh ginger, finely grated
    ¼   c. fresh cilantro leaves, minced
    2   pkg. cream cheese (8 oz. each)
        cranberries for garnish
        cilantro sprigs for garnish
        crackers

Directions:

1. Place cranberries in food processor, and pulse until finely chopped.
2. Transfer to bowl; mix in onion, sugar, lemon juice, jalapeno peppers, ginger, and cilantro.
3. Cover bowl with plastic wrap, and refrigerate for 4 hours until flavor develops.
4. Place cream cheese on serving plate; cover with dip.
5. Garnish with cranberries and cilantro sprigs.
6. Serve with crackers.

Did You Know? . . . .

Did you know that some who oppose consumerism have declared the day after Thanksgiving "Buy Nothing Day" in protest over that day being the beginning of the Christmas shopping season?

Cranberry Red Pretzel Dip

Sweet cranberry sauce is spiced with holiday flavors in this festive dip for pretzels.

Ingredients:

1	can jellied cranberry sauce (16 oz.)
¾	c. sugar
¼	c. white vinegar
1	tsp. ground ginger
1	tsp. ground mustard
¼	tsp. ground cinnamon
⅛	tsp. ground black pepper
1	Tbs. all-purpose flour
1	Tbs. cold water
1	dash red food coloring (optional)

Directions:

1. In saucepan over medium heat, combine cranberry sauce, sugar, vinegar, ginger, mustard, cinnamon, and pepper.
2. Stir until smooth.
3. In small dish stir together flour and cold water.
4. Stir into cranberry sauce.
5. Bring to a boil; cook and stir for 2 minutes.
6. Transfer to serving bowl and stir in red food coloring if using.

Yields: 2 cups.

Did You Know? . . . .

Did you know that since 2003 the public has been invited to vote on the names for the turkeys to be pardoned by the president?

Cranberry Puffs

These cranberry puffs are yummy cranberry and cream cheese-filled wontons. They are a little sweet, a little spicy, and a little salty! A perfect snack for the holidays.

Ingredients:

- ¾ c. fresh cranberries
- 1 jalapeno pepper, stem removed
- ¼ c. sugar
- ½ c. mayonnaise
- 8 oz. cream cheese, softened
- 1 pkg. wonton wrappers (14 oz.)
- 3 c. canola oil for frying

Directions:

1. In food processor combine cranberries, jalapeno pepper, sugar, and mayonnaise; process until smooth.
2. Set aside half of this mixture; transfer remaining mixture to medium bowl.
3. Mix cream cheese into mixture in bowl until well blended.
4. Lay a few wonton wrappers at a time out on clean surface.
5. Spoon about 1 teaspoon cream cheese mixture onto center of each wrapper.
6. Pinch corners together to make triangle shape. (If they do not stick, wet with a little water using your finger.)
7. Set aside on piece of wax paper while assembling remaining puffs.
8. Heat oil in large, deep skillet over medium to medium-high heat.
9. When oil is hot, carefully set 5 to 10 puffs in pan. (Do not crowd pan.)

10. Fry on each side until golden brown.
11. Remove from hot oil using tongs, and place on paper towels to drain.
12. Serve on platter with reserved cranberry relish as dipping sauce.

Yields: 24 appetizers.

Cranberry Cheese Spread

This is a creamy, sweet-tart spread that is ideal for a holiday buffet. It is very colorful and easy to make ahead for your busy day.

Ingredients:

8   oz. cream cheese, softened
½   c. sour cream
2   Tbs. honey
¼   tsp. ground cinnamon
1   can whole-berry cranberry sauce (16 oz.)
⅓   c. slivered almonds, toasted
     assorted crackers

Directions:

1. In small mixing bowl beat cream cheese, sour cream, honey, and cinnamon until smooth.
2. Spread onto serving dish or plate.
3. In another bowl stir cranberry sauce until it reaches spreading consistency; spread over cream cheese mixture and sprinkle with almonds.
4. Cover and refrigerate for 2 to 3 hours.
5. Serve with crackers.

Yields: 12 to 14 servings.

Festive Sausage Cups

These sausage cups are a savory and filling snack. They are very delicious and will disappear quickly.

Ingredients:

    1¼ lb. bulk hot, lean pork sausage
    8   green onions, chopped
    2   Tbs. butter
    ⅔   c. canned mushrooms, chopped
    ⅓   c. thinly sliced stuffed green olives
    ¾   tsp. salt
    ¼   tsp. pepper
    ¼   c. all-purpose flour
    2   c. whipping cream
    1¼ c. shredded Swiss cheese (5 oz.)
       chopped stuffed olives for garnish
       pastry for 9-inch double-crust pie (recipe page 224)

Directions:

1. Preheat oven to 400 degrees F.
2. On lightly floured surface, roll pastry to ⅛-inch thickness.
3. Cut with 2½-inch round cookie cutter.
4. Press onto bottom and up sides of greased miniature muffin cups.
5. Bake for 6 to 8 minutes or until lightly browned.
6. Remove from pans to cool on wire racks.
7. Reduce oven temperature to 350 degrees F.
8. In skillet, brown sausage; drain well and set aside.
9. In same skillet sauté onions in butter until tender.
10. Add mushrooms, sliced olives, salt, and pepper; sprinkle with flour.
11. Add cream; bring to a boil, stirring constantly.
12. Stir in sausage.

13. Reduce heat; simmer until thickened, about 5 to 10 minutes, stirring constantly.
14. Spoon into pastry cups; sprinkle with cheese.
15. Place on ungreased baking sheets.
16. Bake for 10 minutes or until cheese is melted.
17. Garnish with chopped olives; serve hot.

Yields: 4 dozen.

Roasted Chestnuts

Roasted chestnuts are tender and sweet. Add a pinch of salt for a different taste. They are delicious all alone.

Ingredients:

chestnuts

Directions:

1. Preheat oven to 425 degrees F.
2. Place a chestnut on a "deep" dishtowel that is lying flat on a cutting board or countertop. (This will allow the chestnut to "sink" into the dishtowel and keep it from rolling while you make cuts.)
3. Use sharp knife to cut "X" into one side of chestnut to allow steam caused by roasting to escape, otherwise, chestnut will explode.
4. Place each chestnut with cuts facing up onto cookie sheet.
5. Roast for 20 to 30 minutes or until chestnuts are tender, easy to peel, golden brown in color, and shells are beginning to open.
6. Start checking after 20 minutes for shells that are open and insides that look golden.
7. Peel nuts when cool enough to handle. (Hot chestnuts peel easier than cold ones.)

Rye Party Puffs

These appetizers are attractive enough for an elegant party yet also hearty enough to snack on while watching football on television.

Ingredients for puff pastry:

- 1   c. water
- ½   c. butter
- ½   c. all-purpose flour
- ½   c. rye flour
- 2   tsp. dried parsley flakes
- ½   tsp. garlic powder
- ¼   tsp. salt
- 4   eggs
-      caraway seeds

Ingredients for corned beef filling:

- 2   pkg. cream cheese (8 oz. each), softened
- 2   pkg. thinly sliced cooked corned beef (2½ oz. each), chopped
- ½   c. mayonnaise
- ¼   c. sour cream
- 2   Tbs. minced chives
- 2   Tbs. diced onion
- 1   tsp. spicy brown or horseradish mustard
- ⅛   tsp. garlic powder
- 10 sm. stuffed olives, chopped

Directions for puff pastry:

1. Preheat oven to 400 degrees F.
2. In saucepan over medium heat, bring water and butter to a boil.
3. Add flours, parsley, garlic powder, and salt all at once.
4. Stir until smooth ball forms.

5. Remove from heat; let stand for 5 minutes.
6. Beat in eggs one at a time; beat until smooth.
7. Drop batter by rounded teaspoonfuls 2 inches apart onto greased baking sheets.
8. Sprinkle with caraway seeds.
9. Bake for 18 to 20 minutes or until golden.
10. Remove to wire racks.
11. Immediately cut slit in each puff to allow steam to escape; cool.

Directions for corned beef filling:

1. In mixing bowl combine first 8 ingredients; mix well.
2. Stir in olives.
3. Split puffs; add filling.
4. Refrigerate.

Yields: 4½ dozen.

Festive Nut Bowl

Dried cranberries add color and a burst of tartness to the mixed nuts in this easy-to-make nut bowl.

Ingredients:

1   c. macadamia nuts
1   c. cashews
1   c. shelled pistachio nuts
1   c. dried cranberries

Directions:

1. In large bowl mix all ingredients together.
2. Transfer to nice serving dish and serve.

Yields: 4 cups.

Shrimp Cocktail

Shrimp cocktail is always an easy, festive appetizer.

Ingredients for shrimp:

¾   c. water
½   c. white wine
6-10 peppercorns
½   tsp. garlic
1   bay leaf
½-1   lb. shrimp, peeled, deveined
      juice of ½ lemon

Ingredients for sauce:

1   c. mayonnaise
½   c. sour cream
½   c. ketchup
1   Tbs. freshly squeezed lemon juice
½   c. chopped celery
2   Tbs. horseradish
      salt to taste
      dash of cayenne pepper
      dash of hot red pepper sauce

Directions for shrimp:

1. Put all ingredients except shrimp into saucepan, and bring to a boil.
2. Add shrimp and cook until done.
3. Remove shrimp, reserving liquid.

Directions for sauce:

1. Combine all ingredients thoroughly, adding a little of reserved liquid from shrimp.
2. Add shrimp to cocktail sauce and serve.

Spiced Nut Mix

This nut mix can be made ahead to serve in attractive bowls for your Thanksgiving meal.

Ingredients:

- 3   egg whites
- 2   tsp. water
- 2   cans salted peanuts (12 oz. each)
- 1   c. whole blanched almonds
- 1   c. walnut halves
- 1¾ c. sugar
- 3   Tbs. pumpkin pie spice (recipe page 181)
- ¾   tsp. salt
- 1   c. raisins

Directions:

1. Preheat oven to 300 degrees F.
2. In mixing bowl beat egg whites and water until frothy.
3. Add nuts; stir gently to coat.
4. Combine sugar, pie spice, and salt; add to nut mixture and stir gently to coat.
5. Fold in raisins.
6. Spread into 2 greased 15 x 10 x 1-inch baking pans.
7. Bake uncovered for 20 to 25 minutes or until lightly browned, stirring every 10 minutes.
8. Cool.
9. Store in airtight container.

Yields: About 10 cups.

Slow-Cooked Smokies

These little smokies, smothered in barbeque sauce, are popular with children and adults.

Ingredients for smokies:

1   pkg. miniature smoked sausage links (1 lb.)
3½ c. barbeque sauce (see recipe below)
1¼ c. water
3   Tbs. Worcestershire sauce
3   Tbs. steak sauce
½   tsp. pepper

Ingredients for barbeque sauce:

1   bottle ketchup (32 oz.)
1   c. dark molasses
1½ Tbs. red pepper sauce or to taste
1   c. onions, finely chopped
1   med. red bell pepper, finely minced
½   c. lemon juice
1   tsp. garlic powder
2½ Tbs. dry mustard
3   Tbs. white vinegar
¾   c. brown sugar, firmly packed
½   c. water
¼   c. Worcestershire sauce

Directions for smokies:

1. In slow cooker combine all ingredients; mix well.
2. Cover and cook on low for 6 to 7 hours.
3. Serve with a slotted spoon.

Directions for barbeque sauce:

1. Combine all ingredients except water in large, heavy saucepan.
2. Pour water into ketchup bottle and shake, then add to pan.

3. Bring to a boil, stirring constantly.
4. Reduce heat and simmer until onions and bell pepper are very tender, about 2 hours.
5. Stir occasionally.
6. Serve over your favorite meats.

Yields: 8 servings.

Apricot Wraps

This appetizer is very unique and tastes delicious in the sauce.

Ingredients:

1   pkg. dried apricots (14 oz.)
½   c. whole almonds
1   lb. sliced lean, high-quality bacon
¼   c. plum jelly
2   Tbs. soy sauce
    toothpicks

Directions:

1. Preheat oven to 375 degrees F.
2. Fold each apricot around an almond.
3. Cut bacon strips into thirds; wrap a strip around each apricot and secure with a toothpick.
4. Place on 2 ungreased 15 x 10 x 1-inch baking pans.
5. Bake uncovered for 25 minutes or until bacon is crisp, turning once.
6. In small saucepan combine jelly and soy sauce; cook and stir over low heat for 5 minutes or until warmed and smooth.
7. Remove apricots to paper towels; drain.
8. Serve with sauce for dipping.

Yields: 4½ dozen.

Thanksgiving Cheese Ball

Similar to other cheese ball recipes, yet different, this cheese ball, along with a relish tray, is a tasty prelude to Thanksgiving dinner. It may also be served with crackers.

Ingredients:

8   oz. cream cheese, softened
5   oz. sharp cheddar cheese
3   oz. blue cheese, crumbled
2   Tbs. grated onion
1   clove garlic, minced
4   dashes Worcestershire sauce
1   can green olives (2¼ oz.)
¾   c. chopped pecans
     assorted crackers and/or vegetables

Directions:

1. In food processor mix cream cheese, cheddar cheese, blue cheese, onion, garlic, and Worcestershire sauce.
2. Process until well blended.
3. Add olives; pulse into small chunks.
4. Shape mixture into ball; roll in chopped pecans to coat.
5. Wrap in plastic; chill at least 4 hours in refrigerator.
6. Serve with crackers or vegetables.

Did You Know? . . . .

Did you know that the Macy's Thanksgiving Day Parade was suspended from 1942 to 1944 because the rubber and helium were needed for the World War II war effort?

Thanksgiving Delights Cookbook

A Collection of Thanksgiving Recipes
Cookbook Delights Holiday Series Book 11

Beverages

Table of Contents

Page

Did You Know? . . . .

Did you know that some Native American tribes called cranberries Sassamanash?

Chai Tea

I love chai tea, and it is always best when it is homemade with a blend of your favorite spices.

Ingredients:

- 6 oz. milk
- 6 oz. brewed tea
- 2 tsp. sugar
- 1 dash cardamom or ground ginger

Directions:

1. Heat milk.
2. Pour in brewed tea.
3. Stir in sugar and cardamom.

Autumn Tea

This tea blend features flavors we associate with fall— apple, cranberry, and pumpkin pie spice. Serve it either warm or cold.

Ingredients:

- 5 tea bags
- 5 c. boiling water
- 5 c. unsweetened apple juice
- 2 c. cranberry juice
- ½ c. sugar
- ⅓ c. lemon juice
- ¼ tsp. pumpkin pie spice (recipe page 181)

Directions:

1. Place tea bags in large heatproof bowl; add boiling water.
2. Cover and steep for 8 minutes; remove and discard tea bags.
3. Add remaining ingredients to tea; stir until sugar is dissolved.
4. Serve warm or over ice.

Yields: 12 servings.

Cranberry Tea

This colorful tea with its sweet, spicy flavor is a great holiday warmer-upper.

Ingredients:

1   bottle cranberry juice (32 oz.)
2   c. sugar
1   can frozen orange juice concentrate (6 oz.)
1   can frozen lemonade concentrate (6 oz.)
⅓   c. red hot candies
1   cinnamon stick
2   whole cloves

Directions:

1. In 3-quart saucepan combine all ingredients; bring to a boil over medium heat.
2. Boil for 7 minutes, stirring occasionally.
3. Remove cinnamon and cloves.
4. To serve, mix 1 cup concentrate and 2 cups water; heat through.
5. Store concentrate in covered container in refrigerator.

Yields: 18 servings.

Easy Hot Apple Cider

This is a simple spiced apple cider that can be kept warm in a slow cooker so guests can enjoy it all evening. It is great mixed with spiced rum and/or a slice of orange. Leftover cider is good cold, too.

Ingredients:

- 1 bottle apple cider (64 oz.)
- 3 cinnamon sticks
- 1 tsp. whole allspice
- 1 tsp. whole cloves
- 1 Tbs. brown sugar, firmly packed

Directions:

1. In slow cooker combine apple cider and cinnamon sticks.
2. Wrap allspice and cloves in small piece of cheesecloth; add to pot.
3. Stir in brown sugar.
4. Bring to a boil over high heat.
5. Reduce heat and keep warm.

Yields: 8 servings.

Pumpkin Cappuccino

This cappuccino has some surprising fall flavors.

Ingredients:

- ¼ c. minced onion
- 2 oz. butter
- 1 lb. pumpkin purée
- 2 oz. cream sherry
- 1 Tbs. chicken base
- 1 c. heavy whipping cream

1   c. milk
½   tsp. tarragon

Directions:

1. In 2-quart saucepan sauté onions in butter until translucent.
2. Add pumpkin and cook 3 to 4 minutes.
3. Reduce pan with sherry.
4. Add chicken base and stir.
5. Add heavy cream and milk.
6. Season with tarragon to taste.
7. Bring to light boil.
8. Serve in demitasse cups with dollop of frothed milk.

Apple Orchard Punch

This quick and easy punch will be delightful for any fall gathering. Champagne can be used instead of ginger ale for an adult punch.

Ingredients:

1   bottle apple juice (32 oz.), chilled
1   can frozen cranberry juice concentrate (12 oz.)
1   c. orange juice
1½ liters ginger ale
1   red apple

Directions:

1. In large punch bowl combine apple juice, cranberry juice concentrate, and orange juice; stir until dissolved.
2. Slowly pour in ginger ale.
3. Thinly slice apple vertically, forming whole apple slices.
4. Float apple slices on top of punch.

Yields: 24 servings (4 ounces each).

Harvest Coffee Cider

This is an alternative combination to the usual coffee cider.

Ingredients:

- ¼ c. ground coffee, any variety
- ¼ tsp. ground cinnamon
- ¼ c. brown sugar, firmly packed
- 1 c. apple juice or cider
- 3 c. cold water

Directions:

1. Place coffee in filter in brew basket of coffee maker; sprinkle with cinnamon.
2. Place sugar and apple juice in empty pot of coffee maker.
3. Add water to coffee maker; brew.
4. When brewing is complete, stir until well blended.
5. Serve hot and enjoy.

Yields: 4 servings.

Maple Cider Punch

Maple in this fruit punch gives it a holiday flavor.

Ingredients:

- 1 c. orange juice
- 3 Tbs. maple syrup
- 4 c. apple cider, chilled
- 1 c. ginger ale, chilled
  ice cubes

Directions:

1. Pour orange juice in small saucepan; stir in maple syrup.
2. Place over medium heat; bring almost to a boil.
3. Remove from heat, stir once or twice, and let cool to room temperature.
4. Pour apple cider into pitcher; add cooled orange juice and ginger ale; mix well and serve over ice.

Yields: 6 servings.

Cranberry Raspberry Mulled Cider

This cranberry-flavored cider is a great addition to your Thanksgiving meal.

Ingredients:

1   qt. cranberry juice cocktail
1½ c. frozen unsweetened red raspberries, thawed
3   cinnamon sticks (3-in. lengths)
1   tsp. whole cloves
½   vanilla bean, split
½   qt. apple cider

Directions:

1. Slightly mash thawed raspberries.
2. In large saucepan bring cranberry juice, raspberries, cinnamon sticks, cloves, and vanilla bean to a boil over high heat.
3. Lower heat and simmer uncovered for 10 minutes.
4. Strain through tea strainer or sieve, lined with cheesecloth, into large heatproof pitcher.
5. Carefully pour in cider and stir gently; chill.

Yields: About 2 quarts.

Orange Wassail

This is a delicious wassail to serve on your Thanksgiving holiday.

Ingredients:

- 2 qt. orange juice
- 2 qt. apple juice
- 1 qt. cranberry juice cocktail
- 1 can frozen lemonade concentrate, thawed
- 1 cinnamon stick
- 1 Tbs. whole cloves
- 2 oranges, unpeeled, sliced

Directions:

1. Combine first 5 ingredients in large pan; set aside.
2. Insert cloves into orange slices and add to juice mixture.
3. Cook over medium-high heat until thoroughly heated.
4. Serve hot.

Yields: About 5½ quarts.

Pumpkin Juice

This pumpkin juice is unique and a conversation juice to add to your Thanksgiving theme.

Ingredients:

- 2 c. fresh pumpkin, peeled, chopped into chunks
- 2 c. apple juice
- ½ c. pineapple juice
  honey to taste
  cinnamon, ginger, nutmeg, and/or allspice to taste

Directions:

1. Juice pumpkin pieces by squeezing through cheesecloth or using a juicer.
2. Pour pumpkin juice, apple juice, and pineapple juice into blender.
3. Add honey 1 teaspoon at a time to juices, blending thoroughly.
4. Add spices to taste.
5. Chill and serve.

Cranberry Pineapple Cooler

This is a refreshing carbonated cranberry and pineapple cooler.

Ingredients:

2   c. cranberry juice
1   c. pineapple juice
1   c. orange juice
1   jar maraschino cherries (4 oz.)
2   Tbs. lemon juice
1   can or bottle ginger ale (12 oz.)
1   orange, sliced in rounds

Directions:

1. Drain maraschino cherries and reserve juice.
2. In gallon pitcher combine cranberry juice, pineapple juice, orange juice, cherry juice, and lemon juice.
3. Just before serving, slowly add ginger ale; stir to blend.
4. Serve over ice in cups or glasses.
5. Garnish with cherries and orange slices.

Yields: 8 servings.

Pumpkin Pie Smoothie

Pumpkin adds great flavor to this smoothie.

Ingredients:

- 1   can pumpkin purée (15 oz.), chilled
- 1   can evaporated milk (12 oz.), chilled
- 1   c. vanilla-flavored yogurt (8 oz.)
- ¼   c. sugar
- ¼   tsp. pumpkin pie spice (recipe page 181)
- 1   pt. whipping cream, whipped to soft peaks

Directions:

1. Combine pumpkin, evaporated milk, yogurt, sugar, and pumpkin pie spice in blender; cover and blend until mixture is smooth.
2. Pour into glasses or mugs.
3. Top with whipped cream; sprinkle with additional pumpkin pie spice.

Yields: 4 servings.

Spiced Holiday Coffee

This hot holiday coffee has great fragrance and flavor.

Ingredients:

- ⅓   c. ground coffee, any variety
- ½   tsp. ground cinnamon
- ⅛   tsp. ground cloves
- ¼   c. orange marmalade
- 3   c. cold water

Directions:

1. Place coffee, cinnamon, and cloves in filter in brew basket of coffee maker.
2. Place marmalade in empty pot of coffee maker.
3. Add water to coffee maker; brew.
4. When brewing is complete, stir until well mixed.

Yields: 6 servings.

Rosy Citrus Drink

Cranberry juice gets a boost from fresh-tasting citrus juices and a hint of spice in this warm beverage.

Ingredients:

2   c. cranberry juice
1   c. unsweetened grapefruit juice
1   c. orange juice
½   c. sugar
¼   tsp. ground allspice
    apple slices for garnish
    cinnamon sticks for garnish

Directions:

1. In saucepan combine juices, sugar, and allspice; bring to a boil.
2. Serve in mugs, garnished with apple slices and cinnamon sticks if desired.

Yields: 4 servings.

Thanksgiving Citrus Punch

This is a refreshing, easy-to-make punch.

Ingredients:

- 6 c. orange juice, chilled
- 3 c. pineapple juice, chilled
- 1 can frozen lemonade concentrate (12 oz.)
- 2 c. sugar
- 2 qt. ginger ale, chilled
  orange food coloring (optional)
  orange slices for garnish

Directions:

1. In punch bowl combine juices, lemonade, sugar, and food coloring, if desired.
2. Add ginger ale just before serving.
3. Float orange slices on top.

Yields: About 40 servings.

White Hot Chocolate

This white hot chocolate is a fun change of pace from the usual hot chocolate.

Ingredients:

- 6 oz. white chocolate, divided
- ½ c. heavy cream
- 1 qt. milk
- ¼ c. amaretto or, for children, ½ tsp. almond extract

Directions:

1. Coarsely grate ½ ounce white chocolate for garnish; set aside.
2. In small mixing bowl beat heavy cream until stiff peaks form; set aside.
3. Chop remaining chocolate into chunks.
4. In medium saucepan over medium heat, cook chocolate and milk, stirring constantly until chocolate is completely melted.
5. Remove from heat and stir in amaretto or almond extract.
6. Pour into 5 mugs; top with dollop of whipped cream and garnish with reserved white chocolate.

Yields: About 5 servings.

Hot Cranberry Cider

This cider is easy to make and tastes great.

Ingredients:

1   qt. apple cider or apple juice
1   bottle cranberry juice cocktail (32 oz.)
½   c. lemon juice
8   whole cloves
2   cinnamon sticks

Directions:

1. In large saucepan over medium heat, combine all ingredients; bring to a boil, stirring occasionally.
2. Reduce heat and simmer uncovered 10 minutes.
3. Strain out spices and serve warm.

Yields: 2 quarts.

Atole
(Mexican Milk Beverage)

Atole is the historic name in Mexico for this delicious and popular beverage. Made with masa harina, evaporated milk, and sweetened with sugar, this rich and satisfying drink is flavored with vanilla and cinnamon.

Ingredients:

    4¼ c. water, divided
    1   c. masa harina (Mexican corn masa mix)
    2   cans evaporated milk (12 oz. each)
    1   c. sugar
    2   tsp. vanilla extract
    3   cinnamon sticks
       ground cinnamon

Directions:

1. Place 3 cups water and masa harina in blender; cover and blend until smooth.
2. Pour through fine-mesh sieve into medium heavy-duty saucepan; discard solids.
3. Bring to a boil; reduce heat to low.
4. Cook, stirring frequently with wire whisk, for 6 to 8 minutes or until mixture is thickened.
5. Stir in evaporated milk, remaining water, sugar, vanilla extract, and cinnamon sticks.
6. Bring to a boil.
7. Reduce heat to low; cook, stirring frequently, for 5 to 8 minutes or until mixture is thickened.
8. Remove cinnamon sticks.
9. Serve warm sprinkled with ground cinnamon.

Yields: 10 servings.

Thanksgiving Delights Cookbook

A Collection of Thanksgiving Recipes
Cookbook Delights Holiday Series Book 11

Breads and Rolls

Table of Contents

Page

Did You Know? . . . .

Did you know that wild turkeys, while technically the same species as domesticated turkeys, have a very different taste from farm-raised turkeys? Almost all of the meat is "dark" (even the breasts) with a more intense turkey flavor. Older heritage breeds also differ in flavor.

Apple Cider Biscuits

Apple cider adds great fall flavor to these biscuits.

Ingredients:

2   c. all-purpose flour
1   Tbs. baking powder
2   tsp. sugar
½   tsp. salt
⅓   c. cold butter
¾   c. apple cider
⅛   tsp. ground cinnamon

Directions:

1. Preheat oven to 425 degrees F.
2. In bowl combine flour, baking powder, sugar, and salt.
3. Cut in butter until mixture resembles coarse crumbs.
4. Stir in cider just until moistened.
5. Turn onto lightly floured surface and knead 8 to 10 times.
6. Roll out to ½-inch thickness, cut with 2½-inch biscuit cutter, and place on ungreased baking sheet.
7. Sprinkle with cinnamon and pierce tops of biscuits with fork.
8. Bake for 12 to 14 minutes or until golden brown.
9. Serve warm.

Yields: About 1 dozen.

Did You Know? . . . .

Did you know that Norman Rockwell featured a roast turkey as a symbol of prosperity in his painting "Freedom from Want"?

Cornbread

Our family loves cornbread, and this is an easy-to-make recipe that we always double. Any leftovers make great dressing.

Ingredients:

¾ c. cornmeal
1   c. milk
½ c. whole-wheat flour
½ c. all-purpose flour
4   tsp. baking powder
¼ c. sugar
1   egg
⅓ c. oil

Directions:

1. Preheat oven to 400 degrees F.
2. Lightly oil 9-inch square pan.
3. Mix cornmeal and milk in small bowl so cornmeal can soak while preparing remaining ingredients.
4. In large bowl mix together flours, baking powder, and sugar.
5. Mix egg and oil together well, then stir into cornmeal mixture.
6. Add cornmeal mixture to flour mixture; stir to moisten.
7. Pour into prepared pan and bake for 25 minutes or until wooden pick inserted in center comes out clean.

Yields: 16 squares.

Cinnamon-Swirl Raisin Bread

Raisins give a delightful sweetness to this tender potato yeast bread. Cinnamon swirls beautifully through the slices, and it makes terrific toast.

Ingredients:

1½	c. warm milk (110 to 115 degrees F.)
1	c. mashed potatoes (prepared without milk and butter)
¾	c. butter, melted, divided
¾	c. sugar, divided
2	tsp. salt
2	pkg. active dry yeast (¼ oz. each)
½	c. warm water (110 to 115 degrees F.)
6½-7	c. all-purpose flour
1½	c. raisins
1½	tsp. ground cinnamon

Directions:

1. In large bowl combine milk, potatoes, ½ cup plus 2 tablespoons butter, ¼ cup sugar, and salt.
2. In mixing bowl dissolve yeast in warm water.
3. Add potato mixture and 2 cups flour; beat until smooth, then fold in raisins.
4. Stir in enough remaining flour to form soft dough.
5. Turn onto lightly floured surface; knead until smooth and elastic, about 10 minutes.
6. Place in greased bowl, turning once to grease top.
7. Cover and let rise in warm place until doubled, about 1 hour; punch dough down.
8. Turn onto lightly floured surface; divide in half.
9. Roll each portion into a 16 x 8-inch rectangle.
10. Combine remaining ½ cup sugar and cinnamon; sprinkle over rectangles to within ½ inch of edges.
11. Roll up jellyroll style, starting with a short side; pinch seam to seal, and tuck ends under.
12. Place seam side down in two greased 9 x 5 x 3-inch loaf pans.

13. Cover and let rise for 30 minutes or until doubled.
14. Preheat oven to 350 degrees F.
15. Brush loaves with remaining 2 tablespoons melted butter.
16. Bake for 40 to 45 minutes or until golden brown.
17. Remove from pans to wire racks to cool.

Yields: 2 loaves.

Pumpkin Melt-in-Your-Mouth Biscuits

Try these easy-to-make biscuits for your Thanksgiving meal.

Ingredients:

1½ c. all-purpose flour
3   tsp. baking powder
1   tsp. salt
¼   c. sugar
1   tsp. ground cinnamon
½   tsp. ground nutmeg
¼   tsp. ground allspice
⅓   c. butter, cold
¾   c. pumpkin purée
¾   c. milk

Directions:

1. Preheat oven to 450 degrees F.
2. Sift flour into mixing bowl; stir in remaining dry ingredients.
3. Cut in butter with pastry blender until mixture is crumbly.
4. Stir in pumpkin and milk to form soft dough.
5. Roll out on floured surface to ½-inch thickness.
6. Cut out biscuits with biscuit cutter; place on greased baking sheet.
7. Bake for 15 to 20 minutes.

Yields: 24 to 30 biscuits.

Cranberry Nut Bread

This is a quick, festive bread for the Thanksgiving holiday dinner table. It is tart, fragrant, and filled with nuts.

Ingredients:

>   2   c. all-purpose flour
>   1   c. sugar
>   1½ tsp. baking powder
>   1   tsp. salt
>   ½   tsp. baking soda
>   ⅓   c. butter
>   1   egg
>   ¾   c. orange juice
>   1   Tbs. grated orange zest
>   1¾ c. fresh or frozen cranberries
>   1¼ c. chopped walnuts

Directions:

1. Preheat oven to 350 degrees F.
2. Lightly grease 8 x 4-inch loaf pan.
3. In medium bowl mix together flour, sugar, baking powder, salt, and baking soda.
4. Cut in butter until mixture resembles coarse crumbs.
5. In small bowl beat egg, orange juice, and orange zest; blend into dry mixture.
6. Stir in cranberries and walnuts.
7. Transfer to loaf pan.
8. Bake for 65 to 70 minutes or until wooden pick inserted at center comes out clean.
9. Cool in pan 10 minutes; remove to wire rack and cool completely before serving.

Yields: 1 loaf.

Cranberry Yam Bread

Serve this tasty quick bread on Thanksgiving morning with coffee or tea. It also makes a great snack on a chilly autumn or winter day.

Ingredients:

2	lg. eggs, slightly beaten
1⅓	c. sugar
⅓	c. canola oil
1¼	c. fresh yams (sweet potatoes), cooked, mashed or 1 can yams (15 oz.), drained, mashed
1	tsp. vanilla extract
1½	c. all-purpose flour
1	tsp. ground cinnamon
¼	tsp. ground allspice
1	tsp. baking soda
1¼	c. chopped cranberries
	Sweetened Whipped Cream (recipe page 157) or vanilla ice cream for topping

Directions:

1. Preheat oven to 350 degrees F.
2. Coat 9 x 5 x 3-inch loaf pan with nonstick cooking spray and dust with flour.
3. In large bowl combine eggs, sugar, oil, yams, and vanilla.
4. In separate bowl combine flour, cinnamon, allspice, and baking soda; make well in center.
5. Pour yam mixture into well; mix until moistened.
6. Stir in cranberries.
7. Spoon batter into prepared loaf pan.
8. Bake for 1 hour or until wooden pick inserted in center comes out clean.
9. Serve with whipped cream or a scoop of vanilla ice cream.

Yields: 1 loaf.

Pumpkin Gingerbread

This is a wonderfully flavorful and fragrant bread for the holidays.

Ingredients:

3	c. sugar
1	c. vegetable oil
4	eggs
⅔	c. water
1	can pumpkin purée (15 oz.)
2	tsp. ground ginger
1	tsp. ground allspice
1	tsp. ground cinnamon
1	tsp. ground cloves
3½	c. all-purpose flour
2	tsp. baking soda
1½	tsp. salt
½	tsp. baking powder

Directions:

1. Preheat oven to 350 degrees F.
2. Lightly grease two 9 x 5-inch loaf pans.
3. In large mixing bowl combine sugar, oil, and eggs; beat until smooth.
4. Add water and beat until well blended.
5. Stir in pumpkin, ginger, allspice, cinnamon, and cloves.
6. In medium bowl combine flour, soda, salt, and baking powder.
7. Add dry ingredients to pumpkin mixture, and blend just until all ingredients are mixed.
8. Divide batter between prepared pans.
9. Bake until wooden pick inserted near center comes out clean, about 1 hour.
10. Cool for 10 minutes; remove from pans to wire rack to cool completely.

Yields: 2 loaves.

Apple Raisin Quick Bread

Cloves are a subtle but effective complement to the abundant apple pieces in this fruity, golden quick bread.

Ingredients:

  1¼ c. vegetable oil
  4   eggs
  4   tsp. vanilla extract
  3   c. all-purpose flour
  2½ c. sugar
  2   tsp. ground cinnamon
  1½ tsp. salt
  1½ tsp. baking soda
  1   tsp. ground cloves
  ½   tsp. baking powder
  2¼ c. peeled, diced tart apples
  ⅔   c. raisins
  ½   c. chopped nuts

Directions:

  1. Preheat oven to 325 degrees F.
  2. In mixing bowl beat oil, eggs, and vanilla.
  3. Combine flour, sugar, cinnamon, salt, baking soda, cloves, and baking powder; beat into egg mixture.
  4. Stir in apples, raisins, and nuts.
  5. Pour into 2 greased 9 x 5 x 3-inch loaf pans.
  6. Bake for 60 to 70 minutes or until wooden pick inserted near center comes out clean.
  7. Cool for 10 minutes before removing from pans to wire racks to cool completely.

Yields: 2 loaves.

Pumpkin Crescent Rolls

The flavor of these biscuit-like rolls will remind you of pumpkin pie. They make a nice side dish for your Thanksgiving meal.

Ingredients:

> 1¾ c. all-purpose flour
> 1   tsp. baking powder
> ¼   tsp. baking soda
> ¼   tsp. ground nutmeg
> ⅛   tsp. salt
> ¾   c. cooked or canned pumpkin
> 3   Tbs. cooking oil
> 2   Tbs. brown sugar, firmly packed
> 2   tsp. sugar
> ¼   tsp. ground cinnamon

Directions:

1. Preheat oven to 400 degrees F.
2. In medium mixing bowl combine flour, baking powder, soda, nutmeg, and salt.
3. In small mixing bowl combine pumpkin, oil, and brown sugar.
4. Add pumpkin mixture to dry mixture, stirring with fork until combined; form into ball.
5. Line large baking sheet with foil.
6. Turn dough out onto lightly floured surface.
7. Knead dough gently for 10 to 12 strokes.
8. Divide dough in half, then roll each half to a 10-inch circle.
9. Cut each circle into 8 wedges.
10. To shape, begin at wide end of each wedge and loosely roll toward point.
11. Place rolls point side down about 2 inches apart on prepared baking sheet.
12. Curve ends of rolls slightly.
13. Combine sugar and cinnamon; sprinkle over crescents.

14. Bake for 12 to 15 minutes or until golden brown.
15. Serve warm.
16. Make-Ahead Tip: Prepare, bake, and cool rolls.
17. Freeze in freezer container or bag up to 1 month.
18. Wrap frozen rolls in foil and thaw at room temperature for 2 hours.
19. Reheat in oven for 3 to 5 minutes at 375 degrees F.

Yields: 16 rolls.

Maple Corn Bread

It is not necessary to serve maple syrup with this moist corn bread. The maple flavor is baked into it and provides a delicious change of pace from traditional corn bread.

Ingredients:

1¼ c. all-purpose flour
⅓ c. cornmeal
1½ tsp. baking powder
½ tsp. salt
1 egg
¾ c. milk
½ c. maple syrup
3 Tbs. olive oil

Directions:

1. Preheat oven to 400 degrees F.
2. In bowl combine flour, cornmeal, baking powder, and salt.
3. In another bowl beat egg; add milk, syrup, and oil.
4. Stir into dry ingredients just until moistened.
5. Pour into greased 9-inch square baking pan.
6. Bake for 20 to 22 minutes or until wooden pick inserted near center comes out clean.
7. Cool on wire rack for 10 minutes; cut into squares.
8. Serve warm.

Yields: 9 servings.

Soft Onion Breadsticks

Our family loves breadsticks, and these are delicious served warm with butter.

Ingredients:

¾	c. chopped onion
1	Tbs. vegetable oil
2¼	tsp. active dry yeast
½	c. warm water (110 to 115 degrees F.)
½	c. warm milk (110 to 115 degrees F.)
2	eggs
¼	c. butter, softened
1	Tbs. sugar
1½	tsp. salt
3½-4	c. all-purpose flour
2	Tbs. cold water
2	Tbs. sesame seeds
1	Tbs. poppy seeds

Directions:

1. In skillet sauté onion in oil until tender; cool.
2. In mixing bowl dissolve yeast in warm water.
3. Add milk, 1 egg, butter, sugar, salt, and 1 cup flour.
4. Beat on medium speed of electric mixer for 2 minutes.
5. Stir in onion and enough remaining flour to form soft dough.
6. Turn onto floured surface; knead until smooth and elastic, 6 to 8 minutes.
7. Place in greased bowl; turn once to grease top.
8. Cover and let rise in warm place until doubled, about 1 hour.
9. Punch dough down.
10. Let stand for 10 minutes.
11. Turn onto lightly floured surface; divide into 32 pieces.

12. Shape each piece into an 8-inch rope.
13. Place 2 inches apart on greased baking sheets.
15. Cover and let rise for 15 minutes.
16. Preheat oven to 350 degrees F.
17. Beat cold water and remaining egg; brush over breadsticks.
18. Sprinkle half with sesame seeds and half with poppy seeds.
19. Bake for 15 to 22 minutes or until golden brown.
20. Remove to wire racks to cool.

Yields: 32 breadsticks.

Apple Cider Cinnamon Bread (Bread Machine Recipe)

Apple cider flavors this easy-to-make bread.

Ingredients:

1¼ c. apple cider
2 Tbs. butter, softened
3 c. white bread flour
2 Tbs. brown sugar, firmly packed
1 tsp. salt
1 tsp. ground cinnamon
2¼ tsp. active dry yeast

Directions:

1. Place ingredients in bread machine pan in order suggested by manufacturer.
2. Select "Sweet" setting (recommended to use light crust setting) and start machine.

Yields: 1 loaf (1½ pounds).

Whole-Wheat Dinner Rolls

My mom used to make whole-wheat buns for special dinners. They are best served warm right out of the oven.

Ingredients:

2	pkg. active dry yeast (¼ oz.)
2¼	c. warm water (110 to 115 degrees F.)
¼	c. butter
2	eggs
½	c. plus 1 Tbs. sugar
2	tsp. salt
3	c. whole-wheat flour
3½-4	c. all-purpose flour
¼	c. butter, melted

Directions:

1. In large mixing bowl dissolve yeast in warm water; let stand for 5 minutes.
2. Add butter, eggs, sugar, salt, and whole-wheat flour; beat until smooth.
3. Add enough all-purpose flour to form soft dough.
4. Turn onto floured surface; knead until smooth and elastic, about 6 to 8 minutes.
5. Place in greased bowl, turning once to grease top.
6. Cover and let rise in warm place until doubled, about 1 hour.
7. Punch dough down.
8. Divide into four portions; shape each into 12 balls.
9. Place 1 inch apart on greased baking sheets or in 13 x 9 x 2-inch pan if you like them taller and thicker.
10. Cover and let rise until doubled, about 25 minutes.
11. Preheat oven to 375 degrees F.
12. Bake for 11 to 15 minutes or until browned.
13. Brush with butter.

Yields: 4 dozen.

Thanksgiving Delights Cookbook

A Collection of Thanksgiving Recipes
Cookbook Delights Holiday Series Book 11

Breakfasts

Table of Contents

Did You Know?...

Did you know that the juice of red sweet potatoes is combined with lime juice to make a dye for cloth? By varying the proportions of the juices, every shade from pink to purple to black can be obtained.

Cranberry Muffins

These muffins are accompanied by a hot cranberry spread.
They are great for your Thanksgiving menu.

Ingredients for muffins:

2   c. all-purpose flour
1   c. sugar
1½ tsp. baking powder
½   tsp. baking soda
2   tsp. orange zest
1½ tsp. ground nutmeg
1   tsp. ground cinnamon
½   tsp. ground ginger
½   c. butter
¾   c. orange juice
1   tsp. vanilla extract
2   eggs, beaten
1½ c. chopped cranberries
1½ c. chopped walnuts

Ingredients for cranberry spread:

8   oz. Whole-Berry Cranberry Sauce (recipe page 179)
2   Tbs. brown sugar, firmly packed
¼   c. butter

Directions for muffins:

1. Preheat oven to 350 degrees F.
2. Spray or grease a 12-cup and a 6-cup muffin tin.
3. Mix together flour, sugar, baking powder, soda, orange zest, nutmeg, cinnamon, and ginger.
4. Cut in butter.
5. Stir in juice, vanilla, eggs, cranberries, and nuts.
6. Pour into muffin cups; bake for 25 minutes or until brown.

Directions for cranberry spread:

1. In saucepan over low heat, whisk together cranberry sauce, brown sugar, and butter.
2. Cook until heated and smooth.
3. Remove from heat and serve with muffins.

Yields: 18 muffins.

Pumpkin Pecan Oatmeal

Pumpkin and pecans make a nice addition to your morning oatmeal.

Ingredients:

3	c. water
½	tsp. ground cinnamon
¼	tsp. ground nutmeg
⅛	tsp. ground allspice
⅛	tsp. ground cloves
2	c. old-fashioned oats, uncooked
1	c. canned puréed pumpkin
⅓	c. brown sugar, firmly packed
8	oz. vanilla yogurt
3	Tbs. coarsely chopped, toasted pecans

Directions:

1. In medium saucepan bring water and spices to a boil; stir in oats.
2. Return to a boil; reduce heat to medium.
3. Cook 5 minutes or until most of liquid is absorbed, stirring occasionally.
4. Stir in pumpkin and brown sugar; cook 1 minute.
5. Let stand until desired consistency is reached.
6. Spoon oatmeal into bowls; top with yogurt and pecans.

Yields: 4 servings.

Cranberry Pumpkin Waffles

*These waffles are very festive and great for the
Thanksgiving season.*

Ingredients:

¾   c. dried cranberries
2   c. all-purpose flour
2   Tbs. sugar
4   tsp. baking powder
½   tsp. salt
1   tsp. ground cinnamon
1   tsp. ground ginger
1½ c. milk
4   Tbs. unsalted butter
¼   c. olive oil
2   lg. eggs
1   c. canned pumpkin purée

Directions:

1. Plump dried cranberries in hot water to cover for 10
   minutes, then drain.
2. Place flour, sugar, baking powder, salt, and spices in
   large mixing bowl, and stir with fork until blended.
3. Place milk, butter, and oil in small saucepan; heat over
   low heat until butter has melted, then cool slightly.
4. In separate bowl beat eggs with pumpkin purée.
5. Stir in cooled milk mixture.
6. Add to dry ingredients and stir with wooden spoon
   until well combined; stir in cranberries.
7. Preheat waffle iron, and spray with nonstick cooking spray.
8. Add about ½ cup batter. (It takes from ½ cup to ⅔
   cup batter to make 1 waffle, depending on size of
   your waffle iron.)
9. Bake waffles until golden and crisp.
10. Serve hot.

Yields: 4 servings.

Maple Sweet Potato Muffins

This is great recipe for using Thanksgiving leftovers.

Ingredients:

- 1 lg. sweet potato
- 1½ c. all-purpose flour
- 2 tsp. baking powder
- 1 tsp. baking soda
- 1 tsp. ground allspice
- ⅛ tsp. ground cloves
- 1 pinch of salt
- 1 c. maple syrup
- ½ c. milk
- 1 med. egg, beaten

Directions:

1. Cook potato in water at low boil for about 20 minutes, until soft.
2. Allow potato to cool to room temperature.
3. Scoop flesh of potato out of skin, and purée in blender or food processor.
4. Preheat oven to 350 degrees F.
5. In large mixing bowl sift together flour, baking powder, baking soda, spices, and salt.
6. In medium bowl combine syrup, milk, and beaten egg.
7. Add wet ingredients and potato purée to dry ingredients; mix until just combined.
8. Pour evenly into 12 muffin cups prepared with muffin papers or a light coating of cooking spray.
9. Bake for 17 to 20 minutes or until wooden pick inserted into center of largest muffin comes out clean.

Yields: 12 muffins.

Pumpkin Apple Streusel Muffins

Streusel topping makes great muffins.

Ingredients for muffins:

2½ c. all-purpose flour
2 c. sugar
1½ tsp. ground cinnamon
¾ tsp. ground ginger
½ tsp. ground nutmeg
¼ tsp. ground cloves
1 tsp. baking soda
½ tsp. salt
2 eggs, slightly beaten
1 c. canned pumpkin
½ c. vegetable oil
2 c. apples, peeled, cored, finely chopped

Ingredients for streusel topping:

3 Tbs. all-purpose flour
½ c. sugar
½ tsp. ground cinnamon
5 tsp. butter

Directions for muffins:

1. Preheat oven to 350 degrees F.
2. In large bowl combine first 8 ingredients.
3. In medium bowl combine eggs, pumpkin, and oil.
4. Add liquid ingredients to dry ingredients.
5. Stir until just moistened; stir in apples.
6. Spoon batter into greased or paper-lined muffin cups, filling ¾ full.
7. Sprinkle streusel topping over batter.
8. Bake for 35 to 40 minutes or until wooden pick comes out clean.

Directions for streusel topping:

1. In small bowl combine flour, sugar, and cinnamon.
2. Cut in butter until mixture is crumbly.

Pumpkin Apple Waffles

These pumpkin waffles make a nice change of pace.

Ingredients:

1	lg. egg, beaten
2	egg whites, beaten
¼	c. brown sugar, firmly packed
1	c. evaporated milk
2	Tbs. vegetable oil
½	c. canned pumpkin purée
2	tsp. vanilla extract
1	c. all-purpose flour
2	tsp. baking powder
¼	tsp. salt
1½	tsp. ground cinnamon
½	tsp. ground nutmeg
¼	tsp. ground cloves
¼	tsp. ground ginger
½	c. apples, finely diced
¾	c. toasted walnuts

Directions:

1. While waffle iron is heating, beat together egg, egg whites, sugar, milk, oil, pumpkin, and vanilla.
2. Mix dry ingredients and add to egg mixture.
3. Stir just until smooth. (Do not overmix.)
4. Fold in apple and nuts.
5. When waffle iron is hot, spray both top and bottom grids with cooking spray to keep waffles from clinging to iron.
6. Add about ¾ cup batter to center of iron. (Exact amount will vary depending on style and manufacturer of your waffle iron; check instructions.)
7. Close iron and cook until done, 3 to 4 minutes or until waffle stops producing steam.
8. Serve waffles immediately or place in warmed oven to keep hot.

Yields: 6 servings.

Pumpkin Pancakes with Hot Cider Syrup

This makes a nice change of pace from the usual pancake recipes.

Ingredients for pancakes:

2	c. all-purpose flour
2	Tbs. sugar
4	tsp. baking powder
¾	tsp. salt
½	tsp. ground coriander
1	tsp. ground cinnamon
½	tsp. ground nutmeg
1½	c. milk
1	c. canned pumpkin, mashed
4	egg yolks
4	oz. butter, melted
1	Tbs. vanilla extract
4	egg whites, stiffly beaten

Ingredients for syrup:

1½	c. apple cider
1	c. brown sugar, firmly packed
1	c. corn syrup
2	oz. butter
2	Tbs. lemon juice
⅛	tsp. ground cinnamon
⅛	tsp. ground nutmeg
2	apples, peeled, cored, thinly sliced
	grated rind from 1 lemon

Directions for pancakes:

1. In large bowl sift together flour, sugar, baking powder, salt, coriander, cinnamon, and nutmeg.
2. In separate bowl combine milk, pumpkin, egg yolks, butter, and vanilla.
3. Pour combined liquid ingredients into dry ingredients; stir until just blended.
4. Carefully fold in beaten egg whites.
5. Cook pancakes on lightly oiled griddle.

Directions for syrup:

1. In small saucepan combine apple cider, brown sugar, corn syrup, butter, lemon juice, cinnamon, nutmeg, and lemon rind; bring to a boil.
2. Reduce heat and simmer uncovered for 15 minutes.
3. Add apples; heat for several minutes more.
4. Serve over pancakes.

Yields: 6 servings.

Pumpkin Oat Pancakes

Oatmeal adds great texture to these flavorful pancakes.

Ingredients:

1 c. all-purpose flour
1 c. oatmeal
2 Tbs. wheat germ
2 tsp. sugar
2 tsp. baking powder
½ tsp. salt
1 pinch ground cinnamon
1 c. milk
1 egg, lightly beaten
¾ c. canned pumpkin
2 Tbs. vegetable oil

Directions:

1. In bowl combine flour, oatmeal, wheat germ, sugar, baking powder, salt, and cinnamon.
2. In separate bowl combine milk, egg, pumpkin, and oil; stir into dry ingredients just until moistened.
3. Pour batter by ¼ cupfuls onto hot greased griddle; turn when bubbles form on top of pancakes.
4. Cook until second side is golden brown.

Yields: 10 to 12 pancakes.

Pumpkin Spice Bagels

Homemade bagels are extra delicious.

Ingredients:

- 3 c. white bread flour
- 3¼ tsp. active dry yeast
- ½ c. plus 2 Tbs. lukewarm water
- 6 Tbs. brown sugar, firmly packed
- 1 tsp. salt
- ½ c. canned pumpkin purée
- 1½ tsp. ground cinnamon
- 1 tsp. ground cloves
- 1½ tsp. ground nutmeg
- ¾ tsp. ground allspice
- 3 qt. boiling water
- 1 Tbs. sugar
- 1 egg, beaten, for wash
     poppy seeds or sesame seeds for garnish

Directions:

1. In mixer bowl combine 1½ cups flour and yeast.
2. Combine warm water, sugar, salt, pumpkin, and spices; pour over flour mixture.
3. Beat at low speed for 30 seconds, scraping sides of bowl constantly.
4. Beat 3 minutes on high speed.
5. Stir in as much remaining flour as can be mixed in with a spoon.
6. Turn out onto lightly floured surface.
7. Knead in enough remaining flour to make a moderately stiff dough.
8. Continue kneading until smooth and elastic, 6 to 8 minutes.
9. Cover; let dough rest 10 to 15 minutes.
10. Divide into 8 portions.
11. Form balls; gently press thumb through center of ball and slowly stretch into bagel shape.

12. Cover; let rise 20 minutes.
13. While bagels rise, bring 3 quarts water and 1 tablespoon sugar to a rapid boil in large saucepan.
14. Test dough by dropping a piece of dough into boiling water; when bagels are ready to cook, dough will pop up to surface of water right away.
15. Using a slotted spoon, drop 2 to 3 bagels into rapidly boiling water.
16. Boil on each side for 30 seconds.
17. Remove and cool on rack 1 minute; brush with egg and sprinkle with sesame or poppy seeds, if desired.
18. Bake at 400 degrees F. on baking sheet sprinkled with cornmeal until golden, approximately 15 minutes.

Yields: 8 bagels.

Pumpkin Soufflé

Try this pumpkin soufflé. It is very easy to make and flavorful.

Ingredients:

1   c. mashed cooked pumpkin
½   tsp. ground cinnamon
½   c. brown sugar, firmly packed
3   egg whites

Directions:

1. Preheat oven to 350 degrees F.
2. Combine pumpkin, cinnamon, and brown sugar; mix well.
3. Beat egg whites until stiff; fold into pumpkin mixture.
4. Pour into greased 1-quart baking dish and set in pan of hot water.
5. Bake about 40 minutes.

Yields: 4 to 6 servings.

Turkey and Mashed Potato Frittata

Do not throw anything away after holiday meals. Here is tasty recipe for your leftovers.

Ingredients:

4   eggs
8   Tbs. mashed potatoes
1   c. diced cooked turkey meat
⅔   c. cooked vegetables (if you have some), chopped
¾   c. grated cheddar cheese
    olive oil

Directions:

1. Heat small amount of olive oil in large skillet slightly above medium heat.
2. In medium bowl whisk together eggs and potatoes.
3. Pour evenly into skillet.
4. When eggs are nearly half set, spread turkey (and vegetables if you have them) over top evenly.
5. Cover and simmer until egg is fully set.
6. Sprinkle cheese on top; cook 1 minute more until cheese melts.
7. Remove from heat and let sit about 1 minute so cheese will stick to egg.
8. Cut in wedges to serve.

Yields: 2 servings.

Did You Know? . . . .

Did you know that sweet potato leaves and shoots are a good source of vitamins A, C, and B2 (riboflavin)?

Pumpkin Fritters

My mom used to make apple fritters for us when we were kids, and these are also good.

Ingredients:

1	lg. egg
½	c. sugar
½	tsp. salt
1½	c. canned pumpkin purée
1	c. all-purpose flour
¼	tsp. baking soda
1	Tbs. butter, softened
1	tsp. ground cinnamon
½	tsp. ground nutmeg
¼	tsp. ground allspice
¼	tsp. ground cloves
½	tsp. ground ginger
¾	tsp. vanilla extract
	butter and confectioners' sugar for topping

Directions:

1. In small mixing bowl whisk together egg, sugar, and salt until well blended.
2. Add pumpkin purée and continue to mix until well blended.
3. In separate larger bowl sift together flour and baking soda.
4. Add egg mixture to larger bowl along with butter, spices, and vanilla; mix until well combined.
5. Spoon in ¼-cup amounts onto greased griddle over medium-high heat; cook until golden on both sides.
6. Serve warm with a pat of butter and a sprinkling of confectioners' sugar.

Yields: 12 servings.

Whole-Wheat Turkey Breakfast Muffins

Turkey sausage adds great flavor to this easy-to-make breakfast muffin.

Ingredients:

1	lb. turkey breakfast sausage
1	c. all-purpose flour
1	c. whole-wheat flour
2	tsp. baking powder
1	tsp. Italian Seasoning (recipe page 177)
½	tsp. baking soda
¼	c. dry-roasted sunflower seeds
1	c. buttermilk
2	Tbs. vegetable oil
1	lg. egg

Directions:

1. Preheat oven to 400 degrees F.
2. In medium nonstick skillet over medium heat, sauté turkey sausage 5 to 6 minutes or until no longer pink; remove from heat and drain.
3. In large bowl combine turkey, all-purpose flour, whole-wheat flour, baking powder, Italian seasoning, baking soda, and sunflower seeds.
4. In small bowl combine buttermilk, oil, and egg.
5. Fold into flour mixture, stirring just until moistened.
6. Coat 12-cup muffin tin with vegetable cooking spray. (Paper liners may be used in muffin cups for easier clean-up, if desired.)
7. Evenly spoon turkey sausage mixture into each of 12 muffin cups.
8. Bake for 20 to 25 minutes or until wooden pick inserted in center comes out clean.
9. Remove muffins from tin and cool.

Yields: 12 muffins.

Thanksgiving Delights Cookbook

A Collection of Thanksgiving Recipes
Cookbook Delights Holiday Series Book 11

Cakes

Table of Contents

Did You Know? . . . .

Did you know that today only about ⅓ of the top portion of Plymouth Rock remains? In its many journeys around Plymouth, numerous pieces of it were taken and bought and sold.

Butternut Squash Cake

This is a delicious, moist cake that also freezes well.

Ingredients for cake:

- 2 c. sugar
- 2 Tbs. ground cinnamon
- 2 tsp. baking powder
- ¼ tsp. salt
- 4 eggs
- 2 c. all-purpose flour
- 2 tsp. pumpkin pie spice (recipe page 181)
- 2 tsp. baking soda
- 1 c. vegetable oil
- 2 c. butternut squash, cooked, mashed
- 1 c. chopped walnuts

Ingredients for frosting:

- 8 oz. cream cheese, softened
- ½ c. butter
- 1 tsp. vanilla extract
- 1 lb. confectioners' sugar

Directions for cake:

1. Preheat oven to 350 degrees F.
2. Mix all ingredients in large bowl.
3. Transfer to greased and floured 13 x 9 x 2-inch baking pan.
4. Bake for 45 to 50 minutes or until wooden pick inserted in center comes out clean.
5. Allow to cool then frost.

Directions for frosting:

1. Mix ingredients together, adding sugar in stages until desired consistency is reached.
2. Cover cake generously.

Yields: 12 to 15 servings.

Date-Nut Apple Cake

This looks like a standard fruitcake, but the rich, moist texture of apple, dates, raisins, and nuts makes it a very satisfying dessert. Top it with whipped cream or a scoop of ice cream.

Ingredients:

- 1   pkg. chopped dates (8 oz.)
- 1   c. raisins
- 2½ c. all-purpose flour, divided
- ½   c. butter, softened
- 2   c. sugar
- 2   eggs
- 1   tsp. vanilla extract
- 2   tsp. baking soda
- 1   tsp. salt
- 1¾ c. boiling water
- 1   c. peeled, chopped tart apple
- 1¼ c. chopped walnuts
      confectioners' sugar

Directions:

1. Preheat oven to 350 degrees F.
2. In small bowl combine dates and raisins.
3. Add 1 tablespoon flour and toss to coat; set aside.
4. In large mixing bowl cream butter and sugar.
5. Add eggs one at a time, beating well after each addition; beat in vanilla.
6. Combine baking soda, salt, and remaining flour; add to creamed mixture alternately with boiling water.
7. Stir in date mixture, apple, and walnuts.
8. Transfer to greased and floured 10-inch fluted tube pan.
9. Bake for 65 to 70 minutes or until wooden pick inserted near center comes out clean.
10. Cool for 10 minutes before removing from pan to wire rack to cool completely.
11. Dust with confectioners' sugar if desired.

Yields: 10 to 12 servings.

Gingerbread Layer Cake with Cream Cheese Frosting and Candied Pistachios

Dark beer and molasses add rich depth of flavor to this moist and delicious cake.

Ingredients for cake:

1	c. extra stout or dark beer
1	c. mild-flavored (light) molasses
1½	tsp. baking soda
2	c. all-purpose flour
2	Tbs. ground ginger
1½	tsp. baking powder
¾	tsp. ground cinnamon
¼	tsp. ground cloves
¼	tsp. ground nutmeg
⅛	tsp. ground cardamom
3	lg. eggs
½	c. sugar
½	c. dark brown sugar, firmly packed
¾	c. vegetable oil
1	Tbs. peeled, minced fresh ginger

Ingredients for candied pistachios:

1	c. finely chopped pistachios
1	Tbs. light corn syrup
2	Tbs. sugar

Ingredients for frosting:

2	pkg. cream cheese (8 oz. each), room temperature
½	c. unsalted butter, room temperature
¾	tsp. finely grated orange peel
2	c. confectioners' sugar

Directions for cake:

1. Bring stout and molasses to a boil in heavy medium saucepan over high heat.
2. Remove from heat; stir in baking soda.
3. Let stand 1 hour to cool completely.
4. Preheat oven to 350 degrees F.
5. Butter and flour three 8-inch cake pans; line bottoms with parchment paper.
6. Whisk flour and next 6 ingredients in large bowl to blend.
7. Whisk eggs and both sugars in medium bowl to blend.
8. Whisk in oil then stout mixture.
9. Gradually whisk stout-egg mixture into flour mixture.
10. Stir in fresh ginger.
11. Divide batter among prepared pans.
12. Bake until tester inserted into centers of cakes comes out clean, about 25 minutes.
13. Cool cakes in pans 15 minutes.
14. Invert cakes onto racks; cool.
15. Cake can be made 1 day ahead; wrap each cooled cake separately in plastic and keep at room temperature.

Directions for candied pistachios:

1. Preheat oven to 325 degrees F.
2. Line large baking sheet with foil.
3. Mix pistachios and corn syrup in medium bowl.
4. Add sugar and toss to coat.
5. Working quickly so sugar does not melt, spread pistachios on prepared baking sheet.
6. Bake until pistachios are pale golden, about 8 minutes; cool completely.
7. Can be made 1 day ahead; store airtight at room temperature.

Directions for frosting:

1. Using electric mixer, beat cream cheese, butter, and orange peel in large bowl until fluffy.
2. Gradually beat in confectioners' sugar.
3. Chill frosting 30 minutes.

Directions to assemble:

1. Place 1 cake layer, rounded side up, on platter.
2. Spread ¾ cup frosting over.
3. Top with second cake layer, rounded side up, then spread ¾ cup frosting over.
4. Top with third cake layer, flat side up.
5. Spread top and sides of cake with remaining frosting.
6. Sprinkle top of cake with candied pistachios.
7. Can be made 1 day ahead; cover and refrigerate.
8. Bring to room temperature before serving.
9. Cut cake into wedges and serve.

Yields: 10 servings.

Maple Glazed Pumpkin Coffee Cake

This moist pumpkin cake is flavored with the great taste of maple.

Ingredients for cake:

1½ c. all-purpose flour
1   tsp. baking soda
1   tsp. ground cinnamon
¼   tsp. ground allspice
¼   tsp. salt
½   c. unsalted butter, softened
¾   c. light brown sugar, firmly packed
2   lg. eggs

1   c. solid-pack canned pumpkin
⅓   c. maple syrup
1   tsp. vanilla extract

Ingredients for glaze:

1   c. confectioners' sugar
2   Tbs. sour cream
1   Tbs. maple syrup
1   Tbs. fresh lemon juice

Directions for cake:

1. Preheat oven to 350 degrees F.
2. Grease 6½-cup-capacity ring mold.
3. Sift together flour, baking soda, cinnamon, allspice, and salt; set aside.
4. Beat butter and brown sugar with electric mixer until light and fluffy.
5. Add eggs one at a time, mixing well after each addition.
6. Stop mixer and add pumpkin, syrup, and vanilla; mix on low speed.
7. Add dry ingredients; fold in with rubber spatula.
8. Transfer batter to prepared pan.
9. Bake until wooden pick inserted in center comes out clean, 30 to 35 minutes.
10. Cool in pan 5 minutes then carefully loosen from sides of pan with small knife.
11. Invert onto wire rack placed over sheet of wax paper.

Directions for glaze:

1. Sift confectioners' sugar into medium bowl.
2. Add remaining ingredients and mix until smooth.
3. Spoon over warm cake, letting glaze drip down sides; cool completely.

Golden Pumpkin and Apricot Layer Cake

Pumpkin and apricot are a delicious combination in this cake. It is topped with a spiced cream cheese frosting. This is an attractive autumn presentation.

Ingredients for cake:

    2   c. cake flour
    2   tsp. baking powder
    2   tsp. ground cinnamon
    ½   tsp. ground allspice
    ½   tsp. baking soda
    ¼   tsp. salt
    ½   c. apricot purée
    ¾   c. canned solid-pack pumpkin
    ¼   c. buttermilk
    ¾   c. unsalted butter, room temperature
    1½ c. sugar
    3   lg. eggs, room temperature
    2   tsp. vanilla extract

Ingredients for frosting:

    1¼ lb. cream cheese, room temperature (20 oz.)
    2½ c. confectioners' sugar
    ½   c. apricot purée
    ⅓   c. canned solid-pack pumpkin
    ½   tsp. ground cinnamon
    ¼   tsp. ground allspice
        dried apricot cutouts (optional)

Directions for cake:

1. Preheat oven to 350 degrees F.
2. Butter three 9-inch cake pans with 1½-inch-high sides.
3. Dust pans with flour.
4. Sift first 6 ingredients into medium bowl.
5. Blend apricot purée, pumpkin, and buttermilk in small bowl.

6. Using electric mixer, beat butter in large bowl until fluffy.
7. Gradually add sugar, beating until well blended.
8. Add eggs one at a time, beating well after each addition.
9. Mix in vanilla.
10. Mix in dry ingredients alternately with pumpkin mixture, beginning and ending with dry ingredients.
11. Divide batter equally among prepared pans; smooth tops.
12. Bake until tester inserted into center comes out clean, about 25 minutes (cakes will not rise to tops of pans).
13. When cakes have cooled, cut around pan sides to loosen cakes; turn out of pans.

Directions for frosting:

1. Using electric mixer, beat cream cheese and sugar in medium bowl until fluffy.
2. Add apricot purée, pumpkin, and spices; beat until blended.

Directions to assemble:

1. Place one cake layer on platter; spread 1 cup frosting over.
2. Top with second cake layer; spread 1 cup frosting over.
3. Top with third cake layer; spread remaining frosting over sides and top of cake.
4. Place several dried apricots between sheets of plastic wrap.
5. Using rolling pin, roll to flatten.
6. With scissors, cut out leaf shapes from apricots, and arrange on top of cake.
7. Cake can be prepared 1 day ahead; cover with cake dome and refrigerate.
8. Let stand at room temperature 1 hour before serving.

Yields: 10 to 12 servings.

Pineapple Upside Down Cake

These cakes are always attractive and delicious to serve for the holidays.

Ingredients:

½ c. butter
1 c. brown sugar, firmly packed
2 c. cake flour
1 c. sugar
2 tsp. baking powder
¼ tsp. salt
½ c. butter, softened
1 c. milk
2 eggs
1 tsp. vanilla extract
2 cans pineapple slices in syrup (20 oz. each)
  maraschino cherries

Directions:

1. Preheat oven to 375 degrees F.
2. Melt ¼ cup butter in each of two 8-inch square or round baking pans.
3. Drain pineapple; reserve syrup.
4. Sprinkle ½ cup brown sugar over melted butter in each pan.
5. Arrange whole pineapple slices and cherries (with cherries in centers of pineapple slices) over brown sugar in each pan.
6. Cut some of remaining pineapple slices into half circles, then line sides of pans with them (standing up).
7. In bowl combine cake flour, sugar, baking powder, salt, butter, milk, eggs, vanilla, and 4 tablespoons pineapple syrup.
8. Pour ½ of batter into each pan, being careful not to disturb pineapple slices and cherries.

9. Bake for 30 to 35 minutes or until cakes are golden and have pulled away from edges slightly.
10. Remove from oven and allow to stand for a few minutes to set, then turn upside down onto serving dishes; serve while still warm.

Cranberry Cake

The ruby cranberries stay bright and beautiful in this cake, and their tartness is a great combination with your Thanksgiving meal.

Ingredients:

3   eggs
2   c. sugar
¾   c. butter, softened
1   tsp. almond extract
2   c. all-purpose flour
2½ c. cranberries, fresh or frozen, thawed
⅔   c. chopped pecans
     Sweetened Whipped Cream (recipe page 157)

Directions:

1. Preheat oven to 350 degrees F.
2. In mixing bowl beat eggs with sugar until slightly thickened and light in color, about 5 minutes.
3. Add butter and almond extract; beat 2 minutes.
4. Stir in flour just until combined.
5. Stir in cranberries and pecans.
6. Spread in greased 13 x 9 x 2-inch baking pan.
7. Bake for 45 to 50 minutes or until wooden pick inserted near center comes out clean.
8. Serve with whipped cream if desired.

Yields: 16 to 20 servings.

Pumpkin Spice Cake with Hot Caramel Sauce

Plan to serve this cake during the Thanksgiving holiday. It is best served warm and is very delicious.

Ingredients for cake:

1⅓ c. butter, softened
1 c. brown sugar, firmly packed
2 eggs
1 c. cooked or canned pumpkin
1 c. molasses
4 c. all-purpose flour
2 tsp. baking soda
2 tsp. ground cinnamon
2 tsp. ground ginger
½ tsp. ground cloves
¼ tsp. salt
1⅓ c. buttermilk or soured milk
1 c. raisins
1¼ c. chopped walnuts or pecans

Ingredients for hot caramel sauce:

1 c. butter
2½ c. brown sugar, firmly packed
¼ c. corn syrup
1 c. whipping cream

Directions for cake:

1. Preheat oven to 350 degrees F.
2. In large bowl using electric mixer, cream butter and brown sugar until fluffy.
3. Beat in eggs, pumpkin, and molasses until combined.

4. In separate bowl mix together flour, baking soda, spices, and salt.
5. Add flour mixture to creamed mixture alternately with buttermilk until well combined.
6. Stir in raisins and nuts, if desired.
7. Pour into greased 13 x 9 x 2-inch baking pan; smooth top with knife.
8. Bake for 40 to 50 minutes or until wooden pick inserted in center comes out clean.
9. Serve warm with hot caramel sauce.

Directions for hot caramel sauce:

1. Melt butter in medium saucepan over medium-high heat.
2. Stir in brown sugar and corn syrup.
3. Bring to a boil, stirring constantly, until sugar dissolves.
4. Stir in whipping cream; return to boil.
5. Remove from heat.
6. Serve hot over warm cake.

Did You Know? . . . .

Did you know that since 2005 the two turkeys pardoned by the president have been flown first class from Washington, D.C., to Los Angeles on United Airlines so they can be the Grand Marshals of Disneyland's annual Thanksgiving Day parade? They then live the rest of their lives at Disneyland's Frontierland ranch.

Sweet Potato Layer Cake

This is a delicious layer cake with delicious frosting.

Ingredients for cake:

1½ c. vegetable oil
2   c. sugar
4   eggs, separated
1½ c. finely shredded, uncooked sweet potato (about 1 medium)
¼   c. hot water
1   tsp. vanilla extract
2½ c. cake flour
3   tsp. baking powder
1   tsp. ground cinnamon
1   tsp. ground nutmeg
¼   tsp. salt
1¼ c. chopped pecans

Ingredients for frosting:

½   c. butter
1⅓ c. sugar
2   cans evaporated milk (5 oz. each)
4   egg yolks, beaten
3   c. flaked coconut
1¼ c. chopped pecans
2   tsp. vanilla extract

Directions for cake:

1. Preheat oven to 350 degrees F.
2. In mixing bowl beat oil and sugar.
3. Add egg yolks one at a time, beating well after each addition.
4. Add sweet potato, water, and vanilla; mix well.

5. In small mixing bowl beat egg whites until stiff; fold into sweet potato mixture.
6. Combine flour, baking powder, cinnamon, nutmeg, and salt; add to potato mixture.
7. Stir in pecans.
8. Pour into three greased 9-inch round cake pans.
9. Bake for 22 to 27 minutes or until wooden pick inserted near center comes out clean.
10. Cool for 10 minutes before removing to wire racks to cool completely.

Directions for frosting:

1. Melt butter in saucepan; whisk in sugar, milk, and egg yolks until smooth.
2. Cook and stir over medium heat for 10 to 12 minutes or until thickened and bubbly.
3. Remove from heat; stir in coconut, pecans, and vanilla; cool slightly.
4. Place one cake layer on serving plate; spread top with ⅓ of frosting.
5. Repeat layers.

Yields: 10 to 12 servings.

Did You Know? . . . .

Did you know that an attempt was made by Colonel Theophilus Cotton and the townspeople of Plymouth to move the Plymouth Rock in 1774? In the process the rock was split into two halves, and it was decided to leave the bottom portion behind at the wharf with the top half being relocated to the town's meetinghouse. In 1834 the upper portion of the Plymouth Rock was relocated from Plymouth's meetinghouse to Pilgrim Hall. Then in 1880, the top of the rock was moved from Pilgrim Hall back to its original wharf location and the date "1620" was carved into the rock.

Walnut Torte

A hint of citrus complements the rich walnut taste of this lovely three-layer flourless cake. The toasted, chopped walnuts make a great garnish atop the smooth buttercream frosting.

Ingredients for cake:

- 9 eggs, separated
- 1 c. sugar
- ½ c. water
- 1 Tbs. grated orange peel
- 2 tsp. grated lemon peel
- 1 tsp. vanilla extract
- 3 c. finely ground walnuts
- ½ c. dry bread crumbs
- 2 tsp. baking powder
- 1 tsp. ground cinnamon
- 1 tsp. ground cloves
- ½ tsp. salt
- ¼ tsp. cream of tartar

Ingredients for frosting:

- ½ c. shortening
- ½ c. butter, softened
- 1 tsp. vanilla extract
- 4 c. confectioners' sugar
- 3 Tbs. milk
  additional walnuts, toasted, chopped

Directions for cake:

1. Preheat oven to 350 degrees F.
2. Line three 9-inch round cake pans with wax paper; grease paper and set aside.
3. In mixing bowl beat egg yolks until slightly thickened.

4. Gradually add sugar, beating until thick and lemon-colored.
5. Beat in water, peels, and vanilla.
6. Combine walnuts, bread crumbs, baking powder, cinnamon, cloves, and salt; add to batter.
7. Beat until smooth.
8. In another mixing bowl beat egg whites and cream of tartar until stiff peaks form.
9. Fold half into batter then fold in remaining whites.
10. Pour into prepared pans.
11. Bake for 20 to 25 minutes or until wooden pick inserted near center comes out clean.
12. Cool for 10 minutes before removing from pans to wire racks.
13. Carefully remove wax paper.

Directions for frosting:

1. In mixing bowl cream shortening and butter.
2. Beat in vanilla.
3. Gradually beat in sugar.
4. Add milk; beat until light and fluffy.
5. Spread frosting between layers and over top and sides of cake.
6. Garnish with toasted walnuts.

Yields: 12 to 15 servings.

Did You Know? . . . .

Did you know that in parts of Canada, pumpkin pie is commonly served with maple syrup instead of whipped cream?

Swedish Spice Cake
(Kryddkaka)

Try this flavorful spice cake—Swedish style.

Ingredients:

2   eggs
1   c. sugar
1¼ c. all-purpose flour
2   tsp. ground cinnamon
1   tsp. ground cardamom
½   tsp. ground cloves
1½ tsp. baking powder
⅓   c. water
¼   c. butter
1   Tbs. bread crumbs

Directions:

1. Preheat oven to 350 degrees F.
2. Beat eggs until very light and fluffy.
3. Add sugar gradually while beating.
4. Sift together flour, spices, and baking powder.
5. Fold into egg mixture gently, so as not to deflate eggs.
6. In small saucepan heat butter and water over low heat until butter has melted.
7. Once butter melts, bring to a boil and add to batter while still boiling hot; combine thoroughly.
8. Butter 7¾-inch tube pan and sprinkle evenly with bread crumbs.
9. Pour cake batter into pan.
10. Bake for 45 to 50 minutes or until cake tests done.
11. Serve unfrosted or with confectioners' icing.
12. Serving suggestion: Slice and serve with fruit and fruit syrup topped with whipped cream.

Thanksgiving Delights Cookbook

A Collection of Thanksgiving Recipes
Cookbook Delights Holiday Series Book 11

Candies

Table of Contents

Did You Know? . . . .

Did you know that turkeys were a favorite domesticated animal among the Aztecs and were taken to Europe by the Spanish?

Almond Candy Jewels

These are easy to make, and they make a nice holiday gift.

Ingredients:

⅓ c. butter
2   c. slivered almonds
⅓ c. sugar
2   Tbs. light corn syrup
½ c. of one of the following:
     semisweet real chocolate morsels
     butterscotch morsels
     vanilla morsels
     toffee chips
     chopped red and green candied cherries

Directions:

1. Line large baking sheet with wax paper; set aside.
2. Melt butter in 10- or 12-inch skillet until sizzling; add almonds, sugar, and corn syrup.
3. Cook over medium heat, stirring constantly with wooden spoon until sugar and nuts are golden brown, 4 to 9 minutes. (Watch closely to prevent burning.)
4. Immediately remove from heat; sprinkle with desired topping. (Do not stir.)
5. Working quickly, drop level tablespoonfuls of almond mixture onto prepared baking sheet, forming mounds.
6. Refrigerate until firm, about 45 minutes.
7. Place individual clusters in paper candy cups or on squares of colored foil.
8. Store in airtight container at room temperature.

Yields: 30 candies.

Almond Coconut Toffee

Almonds and coconut combine to make a delicious toffee candy. Toffee is a great holiday treat and makes a great gift.

Ingredients:

1 c. sugar
½ c. butter
¼ c. light corn syrup
¼ c. water
1½ c. slivered almonds, divided
1½ c. flaked coconut, divided
4 oz. semisweet chocolate, coarsely chopped

Directions:

1. Lightly grease baking sheet.
2. Bring sugar, butter, corn syrup, and water to a boil in saucepan over high heat, stirring occasionally.
3. Cook 14 to 16 minutes or until mixture changes from golden yellow to golden brown.
4. Remove from heat; stir in 1¼ cup almonds and 1¼ cups coconut.
5. Coarsely chop remaining almonds; set aside.
6. Spread mixture evenly on prepared baking sheet.
7. Sprinkle chocolate over toffee mixture; let stand 1 minute to soften chocolate then spread to cover toffee evenly.
8. Sprinkle remaining almonds and coconut evenly over melted chocolate.
9. Refrigerate for at least 30 minutes.
10. Break into pieces.
11. Store in airtight container.

Yields: 1½ pounds.

Buttermilk Pralines

These sweet pralines, slightly tart from the buttermilk, can be eaten whole or crushed and sprinkled over ice cream or other desserts.

Ingredients:

- 3 c. sugar
- 1 c. buttermilk
- 1 tsp. baking soda
- ¼ tsp. salt
- 1 tsp. vanilla extract
- 2 tsp. butter
- 2 c. pecan halves

Directions:

1. In medium saucepan mix together sugar, buttermilk, baking soda, and salt.
2. Cook over medium heat until a bit of mixture forms a soft ball when dropped into cold water (soft-ball stage).
3. Remove from heat and stir in vanilla, butter, and pecans; return to heat.
4. Cook, stirring constantly, scraping bottom of pan with spoon, until mixture again reaches soft-ball stage.
5. Remove from heat.
6. While still hot, drop mixture by teaspoonfuls onto wax paper.
7. When cool, serve whole or crush into bite-size pieces.

Yields: About 3 dozen pralines or 5 cups crushed pralines.

Candy Corn Fudge

This makes a decorative Thanksgiving fudge.

Ingredients:

- 1 pkg. vanilla or white chocolate chips (12 oz.)
- 2 containers vanilla frosting (16 oz. each)
- 1 pkg. butterscotch flavored chips (10 oz.), melted
- ⅛ tsp. or more yellow food coloring, divided
- ⅛ tsp. or more red food coloring
- 48 pieces candy corn

Directions:

1. Line 13 x 9 x 2-inch pan with foil, leaving about 2 inches of overhang on each end; butter foil.
2. Melt vanilla chips.
3. In large bowl combine melted vanilla chips and half the frosting; mix well.
4. Spread ⅓ of mixture in prepared pan.
5. Combine melted butterscotch chips and remaining frosting in another large bowl; mix well.
6. Add enough yellow and red food coloring to turn mixture orange; stir until well blended.
7. Spread orange mixture over white layer in pan.
8. If remaining white mixture has hardened, heat in microwave until just melted and smooth, stirring occasionally.
9. Add enough yellow food coloring to turn mixture yellow; stir until well blended.
10. Spread over orange layer in pan.
11. Refrigerate 1 hour or until firm.
12. Use foil to lift fudge from pan.
13. Turn white side up and carefully peel off foil.
14. Cut into 48 pieces.
15. Press a candy corn into center of each piece.
16. Store in refrigerator.

Yields: 48 pieces.

Chocolate Caramels

Homemade chocolate caramels will liven up any party.

Ingredients:

- 1 c. butter
- 1 c. sugar
- 1 c. dark brown sugar, firmly packed
- 1 c. light corn syrup
- 1 can sweetened condensed milk (14 oz.)
- 1 bar unsweetened chocolate (2 oz.)
- 1 tsp. vanilla extract

Directions:

1. Line 8-inch square baking pan with foil; grease.
2. Combine butter, sugar, brown sugar, and corn syrup in heavy-duty medium saucepan.
3. Cook over medium heat, stirring constantly, until mixture comes to a boil and butter is melted.
4. Add sweetened condensed milk and chocolate; stir constantly until chocolate is melted.
5. Cook over medium-low heat, stirring frequently, for 25 to 35 minutes or until mixture reaches 245 degrees F. on candy thermometer.
6. Remove from heat; stir in vanilla.
7. Immediately pour into prepared pan; cool.
8. Lift from pan; remove foil.
9. Cut into 1-inch squares and wrap individually in plastic wrap, twisting ends.
10. Store at room temperature; use within 7 to 10 days.
11. Note: If caramels become too firm to cut, soften slightly in microwave oven on medium-low (30%) power for about 1 minute or warm in oven at 200 degrees F. for about 5 minutes.

Yields: 64 pieces.

Indian Corn on a Stick

This fun autumn treat looks like colorful Indian corn. Wrapped in cellophane and tied with raffia, these popcorn treats would make a perfect favor for your Thanksgiving table.

Ingredients:

¾ c. butter
60 lg. marshmallows
3 qt. popped popcorn
¼ c. peanuts or other coarsely chopped nuts
¼ c. shredded coconut
1 c. chopped dried fruits (cranberries, apricots, pineapple, apples, raisins, etc.)
skewers, wooden sticks, or dowels

Directions:

1. Melt butter and marshmallows in saucepan over low heat.
2. Pour over popped popcorn and stir in nuts, coconut, and dried fruits.
3. When cool enough to handle, butter hands and mold popcorn mixture into ear-of-corn shapes about 6 inches long.
4. Place on greased cookie sheet or wax paper to set.
5. Immediately, while marshmallow is still sticky, place a few pieces of nuts and dried fruits on the "ears of corn" to resemble colorful kernels of corn.
6. Insert skewer, wooden stick, or dowel in end of each "ear of corn."
7. Let cool.
8. When marshmallow is set, wrap with cellophane, and tie with raffia bow if desired.

Yields: 6 or 7 servings.

Chocolate Truffles

These are easy-to-make truffles that make great gifts.

Ingredients:

> 3 c. semisweet chocolate chips (18 oz.)
> 1 can sweetened condensed milk (14 oz.)
> 1 Tbs. vanilla extract
>   chopped flaked coconut
>   chocolate sprinkles
>   colored sprinkles
>   baking cocoa
>   finely chopped nuts

Directions:

1. In microwave-safe bowl, heat chocolate chips and milk at 50% power until chocolate is melted.
2. Stir in vanilla.
3. Chill for 2 hours or until mixture is easy to handle.
4. Shape into 1-inch balls.
5. Roll in coconut, sprinkles, cocoa, or nuts if desired.

Yields: About 4 dozen.

Candy Nuts

These candied nuts are easy to make and delicious. They keep well, so they can be made ahead.

Ingredients:

> 1½ c. cashews, peanuts, whole almonds, or pecan halves (raw or roasted)
> ½ c. sugar
> 2 Tbs. butter
> ½ tsp. vanilla extract

Directions:

1. Line baking sheet with foil; butter foil and set aside.
2. In 10-inch heavy skillet combine nuts, sugar, butter, and vanilla.
3. Cook over medium-high heat, shaking skillet occasionally, until sugar begins to melt. (Do not stir.)
4. Reduce heat to low; continue cooking until sugar is golden brown, stirring occasionally.
5. Remove skillet from heat; pour nut mixture onto prepared baking sheet.
6. Cool completely and break into clusters.
7. Store tightly covered in refrigerator for up to 3 weeks.

Yields: 12 servings.

Nut Candy

This is an extra-delicious candy treat that is easy to make.

Ingredients:

1 pkg. chocolate chips (12 oz.)
2 c. mixed nuts, peanuts, or cashews

Directions:

1. Melt chocolate chips in double boiler.
2. Stir in your choice of nuts.
3. Drop by teaspoonfuls onto wax paper.
4. Allow to cool and harden.

Yields: 1 pound.

Cranberry Nut Fudge

This is a colorful and delicious holiday fudge.

Ingredients:

1	pkg. white chips (12 oz.)
1	jar marshmallow cream (7 oz.)
1	c. dried sweetened cranberries
½	tsp. orange extract
⅓	c. evaporated milk
⅓	c. cranberry juice concentrate
2½	c. sugar
¼	c. butter
1	c. chopped walnuts

Directions:

1. Line 9-inch square pan with aluminum foil; set aside.
2. Place white chips, marshmallow cream, cranberries, and orange extract in 3-quart saucepan; set aside.
3. Heat milk and cranberry juice in saucepan over medium heat until warm; add sugar.
4. Raise heat to medium-high and bring to a rolling boil, stirring constantly with wooden spoon.
5. Continue to boil for 8 full minutes, or if using a candy thermometer, continue boiling until mixture reaches 235 degrees F., but do not exceed 9 minutes rolling boil total.
6. Remove from heat and add butter.
7. Stir until dissolved but no more than 30 seconds.
8. Pour hot mixture over white chips, orange extract, and marshmallow cream without scraping sides of hot saucepan; mix until chips are melted.
9. Stir in chopped walnuts.
10. Mix thoroughly and transfer to prepared pan.
11. Cool at room temperature.
12. Chill in refrigerator prior to cutting.
13. Remove from pan, remove foil, and cut into squares.

Honey Walnut Caramels

Drop one of these caramels into a cup of hot coffee or tea, or just enjoy this delicious treat on its own.

Ingredients:

- 1 c. half-and-half or evaporated milk
- 1 c. honey
- 2 tsp. all-purpose flour
- ½ tsp. salt
- ¼ c. butter
- 1 tsp. vanilla extract
- 1 c. chopped walnuts

Directions:

1. Butter 8 x 4-inch or 9 x 5-inch loaf pan.
2. In heavy 1½-quart saucepan over medium heat, combine half-and-half, honey, flour, and salt.
3. Stir to dissolve sugar and any lumps that form from the flour.
4. Add butter; bring to a boil over medium heat, stirring constantly.
5. Cook, stirring frequently, to firm-ball stage (248 degrees F. on candy thermometer).
6. Remove from heat; stir in vanilla and walnuts.
7. Pour into buttered pan.
8. Cool and cut into squares.
9. Wrap each piece individually in plastic.
10. Store in airtight container.

Yields: About 1 pound.

Did You Know? . . . .

Did you know that in 2004 the two turkeys pardoned by the President were named Biscuit and Gravy?

Macadamia Nut Fudge

This makes a great holiday fudge.

Ingredients:

    2   c. sugar
    2   sq. unsweetened chocolate (1 oz. each)
    1   pinch salt
    1   c. light cream or half-and-half
    2   Tbs. light corn syrup
    ¼   c. butter
    1¼ c. coarsely chopped macadamia nuts
    1   tsp. vanilla extract

Directions:

1. Butter 9 x 5-inch loaf pan.
2. Combine sugar, chocolate, and salt in 3-quart microwave-safe mixing bowl or casserole.
3. Stir in cream and corn syrup; add butter.
4. Cover and microwave on high for 5 minutes; mix well.
5. Microwave uncovered 10 to 14 minutes or until soft-ball stage is reached (234 to 240 degrees F.).
6. Cool mixture, without stirring, to 120 degrees on edges.
7. Add nuts and vanilla.
8. Beat until mixture is thick and creamy and starts to lose its shine.
9. Quickly spread in pan. (If fudge is too thick to spread, stir in a few drops of cream.)
10. Cool completely.
11. Cut in 1-inch squares.
12. Store in airtight container in cool, dry place up to 2 weeks.

Yields: 1 pound.

Pumpkin Fudge

This makes a great autumn fudge.

Ingredients:

- 1 tsp. butter
- 2 c. sugar
- ⅓ c. evaporated milk or cream
- 3 Tbs. pumpkin purée
- ¼ tsp. cornstarch
- ¼ tsp. (rounded) pumpkin pie spice (recipe page 181)
- ½ tsp. vanilla extract
- 1 c. chopped walnuts

Directions:

1. Line 8 x 8 x 1½-inch square pan with aluminum foil, allowing foil to hang over edges of pan.
2. Grease pan with 1 teaspoon butter.
3. Place sugar, milk, pumpkin, cornstarch, and pumpkin pie spice in saucepan; cook quickly, stirring constantly, until boiling.
4. Cover and cook 2 to 3 minutes.
5. Uncover, reduce heat, and cook until mixture reaches soft-ball stage (234 degrees F.) or when small amount dropped into chilled water forms a ball and flattens when picked up.
6. Remove from heat and place in mixing bowl.
7. Cool to 110 degrees F.
8. Add vanilla and beat with mixer until smooth and creamy; add nuts, if desired.
9. Pour into prepared baking pan.
10. When firm, remove fudge from pan, peel away foil, and cut into squares.

Yields: 1½ pounds.

Turkey Candies

These turkey treats are fun and easy to make for Thanksgiving.

Ingredients:

- 15 chocolate candy stars
- 15 caramels, unwrapped
- 15 scalloped, chocolate-frosted shortbread cookies
- 15 pieces candy corn

Directions:

1. Place each chocolate candy star point side up on work surface.
2. Place one caramel on wax paper and microwave on high for about 10 seconds so it is slightly softened.
3. Place softened caramel on tip of chocolate candy star, pressing down so they stick together.
4. To make tail, press chocolate cookie, striped side facing forward, firmly against soft caramel to stand upright.
5. Press candy corn on top of caramel to give shape of turkey's beak.
6. Repeat process to make remaining turkey treats.

Yields: 15 turkey candies.

Did You Know? . . . .

Did you know that Samoset was the first Native American to make contact with the Pilgrims and that he brought Squanto a few days later because he spoke better English?

Thanksgiving Delights Cookbook

A Collection of Thanksgiving Recipes
Cookbook Delights Holiday Series Book 11

Cookies

Table of Contents

Did You Know? . . . .

Did you know that some animal welfare groups say that turkeys each have unique personalities and make wonderful companions?

Chocolate Candy Corn Sugar Cookies

Children always seem to love these candy corn sugar cookies that are great autumn treats.

Ingredients:

4   Tbs. butter, very soft (no substitutions)
½   c. sugar
1   egg yolk
¼   tsp. vanilla extract
¼   tsp. baking powder
¼   tsp. salt
½   c. all-purpose flour
¼   c. baking cocoa
36 pieces candy corn

Directions:

1. Preheat oven to 350 degrees F.
2. Place butter and sugar in medium bowl; beat well using wooden spoon.
3. Add egg yolk, vanilla, baking powder, and salt; mix until combined.
4. Add flour and cocoa; mix until dough forms.
5. Scoop out level teaspoons of dough; form into balls.
6. Place dough on cookie sheet and bake for 10 to 12 minutes or until edges are firm and cookies feel dry to the touch.
7. Remove pan from oven and immediately press 1 candy corn into center of each cookie.
8. Allow cookies to cool on pan for 1 minute before removing to wire rack to cool completely.
9. Vanilla Variation: Simply omit cocoa and increase flour to ¾ cup; otherwise, proceed same as above.

Yields: 3 dozen.

Cranberry Pecan Bars

These cranberry pecan bars add color and flavor to your holiday table.

Ingredients:

- ¼ c. butter, softened
- 1 c. all-purpose flour
- ½ c. brown sugar, firmly packed
- 1 tsp. finely grated orange peel
- ½ c. orange juice
- 1 egg
- ½ tsp. baking powder
- ¼ tsp. baking soda
- 1 c. chopped pecans
- ¾ c. chopped cranberries
-    confectioners' sugar

Directions:

1. Preheat oven to 350 degrees F.
2. In mixing bowl beat butter with electric mixer on medium speed for 30 seconds.
3. Add about ½ of the flour, the brown sugar, orange peel, ½ of the orange juice, then egg, baking powder, and baking soda; beat until thoroughly combined.
4. Beat in remaining flour and orange juice.
5. Stir in pecans and cranberries.
6. Spread onto ungreased 11 x 7 x 2-inch baking pan.
7. Bake for 25 minutes or until wooden pick inserted near center comes out clean.
8. Cool in pan on wire rack.
9. Sift confectioners' sugar over top, and cut into bars.

Cranberry-Walnut Rugelach

These are rich, flavorful roll ups.

Ingredients:

- 1 c. unsalted butter, room temperature
- 8 oz. cream cheese, room temperature
- ¼ c. sugar
- 2 egg yolks
- 1 tsp. vanilla extract
- ½ tsp. salt
- 2 c. all-purpose flour
- ½ c. apricot jam
- 1 c. dried cranberries
- 1 c. finely chopped walnuts
- ¼ c. milk
- 3 Tbs. sugar

Directions:

1. Blend butter, cream cheese, and sugar in bowl until smooth and creamy, 2 minutes.
2. Stir in egg yolks, vanilla, and salt.
3. Stir in flour until smooth dough forms.
4. Divide into fourths then shape into disks.
5. Wrap each disk in plastic wrap.
6. Refrigerate 4 hours or overnight.
7. Position rack in top ⅓ of oven.
8. Preheat oven to 350 degrees F.
9. Line 2 baking sheets with foil; grease foil.
10. Roll out one disk into 8-inch round.
11. Spread with 2 tablespoons apricot jam.
12. Sprinkle with ¼ c. dried cranberries and about ¼ cup nuts; cut disk into 8 wedges.
13. Starting at outside edge, roll up each triangle.
14. Place on sheet, spacing 1 inch apart.
15. Repeat with remaining dough and filling.
16. Brush each pastry with milk; sprinkle with sugar.
17. Bake for 25 to 30 minutes or until lightly browned.
18. Remove to wire rack to cool.

Crisp Anise Cookies

These are a great accompaniment to cold milk, hot coffee, or your favorite tea.

Ingredients:

    1 ½ c. all-purpose flour
    ¾   tsp. baking powder
    ¼   tsp. salt
    ½   c. unsalted butter, room temperature
    ⅓   c. plus 2 Tbs. sugar, divided
    1   lg. egg yolk
    2   Tbs. brandy
    ½   tsp. aniseed, toasted

Directions:

1. Preheat oven to 325 degrees F.
2. Toast aniseed in dry skillet over medium heat until fragrant, about 1 minute.
3. Sift flour, baking powder, and salt into small bowl.
4. Beat butter and ⅓ cup sugar in large bowl until light, then beat in egg yolk, brandy, and aniseed.
5. Add dry ingredients, and beat just until smooth dough forms.
6. Spread remaining 2 tablespoons sugar on small plate.
7. Roll out dough on lightly floured surface to ¼-inch thickness; using 2-inch cookie cutter, cut out cookies.
8. Gather scraps, reroll on lightly floured surface, and cut out more cookies.
9. Place cookies one at a time on sugar on plate; transfer cookies, sugar side up, to 2 ungreased baking sheets.
10. Bake until bottom and edges are golden, about 20 minutes; transfer cookies to rack and cool.
11. Cookies can be prepared 3 days ahead.
12. Store in airtight container at room temperature.

Yields: 24 cookies.

Frosted Pumpkin Walnut Cookies

These make an old-fashioned, soft cookie.

Ingredients for cookies:

½   c. butter, softened
1½ c. brown sugar, firmly packed
2   eggs
1   c. pumpkin purée
½   tsp. vanilla extract
½   tsp. lemon extract
2½ c. all-purpose flour
1   Tbs. baking powder
½   tsp. salt
2   tsp. pumpkin pie spice (recipe page 181)
1   c. walnuts, chopped

Ingredients for frosting:

¼   c. butter, softened
2¼ c. confectioners' sugar, sifted
2   Tbs. milk
¾   tsp. maple extract

Directions for cookies:

1. Preheat oven to 375 degrees F.
2. Cream butter; gradually add brown sugar, beating well at medium speed of electric mixer.
3. Add eggs one at a time, beating after each addition.
4. Stir in pumpkin and flavorings.
5. Combine flour, baking powder, salt, and pumpkin pie spice; gradually add to creamed mixture, mixing well.
6. Stir in walnuts.
7. Drop dough by teaspoonfuls 2 inches apart onto greased cookies sheets.
8. Bake for 12 minutes.
9. Remove to wire racks to cool.

Directions for frosting:

1. Cream butter; gradually add 1 cup confectioners' sugar, beating well at medium speed of electric mixer.
2. Add remaining sugar alternately with milk, beating until smooth enough to spread.
3. Add maple extract; beat well.
4. Frost cooled cookies.

Yields: 7½ dozen cookies; about 1 cup frosting.

Apricot Almond Chewies

These apricot almond balls make a great change of pace.

Ingredients:

    4   c. finely chopped dried apricots (about 1 lb.)
    4   c. flaked coconut or coconut macaroon crumbs
        (about 21 macaroons)
    2   c. slivered almonds, toasted, finely chopped
    1   can sweetened condensed milk (14 oz.)
        whole almonds

Directions:

1. In large bowl combine all ingredients except whole almonds.
2. Chill 2 hours.
3. Shape chilled dough into 1-inch balls.
4. Top each with whole almond.
5. Store leftovers tightly covered in refrigerator.

Yields: About 7 dozen cookies.

Pumpkin Carrot Swirl Bars

These bars are attractive, moist, and easy to make.

Ingredients for bars:

2   c. all-purpose flour
2¼ tsp. pumpkin pie spice (recipe page 181)
2   tsp. baking powder
1   tsp. baking soda
⅓   c. butter, softened
1   c. sugar
½   c. brown sugar, firmly packed
2   lg. eggs
2   lg. egg whites
1   can pumpkin purée (15 oz.)
1   c. finely shredded carrot
    cream cheese topping (recipe follows)

Ingredients for topping:

4   oz. cream cheese, softened
¼   c. sugar
1   Tbs. milk

Directions for bars:

1. Preheat oven to 350 degrees F.
2. Grease 15 x 10-inch jellyroll pan.
3. Combine flour, pumpkin pie spice, baking powder, and baking soda in small bowl.
4. Beat butter and sugars in large mixing bowl until crumbly.
5. Add eggs, egg whites, pumpkin, and carrot; beat until well blended.
6. Add flour mixture; mix well.
7. Spread into prepared pan.

8. Drop teaspoonfuls of cream cheese topping over batter; swirl mixture with spoon.
9. Bake 25 minutes or until wooden pick inserted in center comes out clean.
10. Cool completely in pan on wire rack.

Directions for topping:

1. Combine all ingredients in small mixing bowl until thoroughly combined.

Yields: About 4 dozen bars.

Maple Meltaways

These cookies are easy to make, and they disappear quickly.

Ingredients:

2   c. all-purpose flour
1   c. butter, softened
¾   c. sugar
1½ tsp. maple extract
¼   tsp. salt
⅔   c. pecan halves

Directions:

1. Preheat oven to 350 degrees F.
2. Combine first 5 ingredients in large bowl; beat until fluffy.
3. Drop dough by rounded teaspoonfuls onto ungreased cookie sheet.
4. Press pecan half in center of each cookie.
5. Bake for 10 minutes or until lightly brown.
6. Cool cookies on wire rack.

Yields: 4 dozen.

Pumpkin Chip Cookies

These golden cake-like cookies will disappear quickly from your dessert trays. The subtle pumpkin and cinnamon flavors pair nicely with chocolate chips.

Ingredients:

1½ c. butter, softened (no substitutes)
2   c. brown sugar, firmly packed
1   c. sugar
1   can solid-pack pumpkin (15 oz.)
1   egg
1   tsp. vanilla extract
4   c. all-purpose flour
2   c. quick-cooking oats
2   tsp. baking soda
2   tsp. ground cinnamon
1   tsp. salt
2   c. semisweet chocolate chips (12 oz.)

Directions:

1. Preheat oven to 350 degrees F.
2. In large mixing bowl cream butter and sugars.
3. Beat in pumpkin, egg, and vanilla.
4. Combine flour, oats, baking soda, cinnamon, and salt; gradually add to creamed mixture.
5. Stir in chocolate chips.
6. Drop by tablespoonfuls 2 inches apart onto ungreased baking sheets.
7. Bake for 10 to 12 minutes or until lightly browned.
8. Remove to wire racks to cool.

Yields: 10 dozen.

Pumpkin Bars with Crumb Topping

These bars are easy to make and a nice variety with the crumb topping.

Ingredients for crust and topping:

    1½ c. quick-cooking oats
    1¼ c. all-purpose flour
    ¾   c. light brown sugar, firmly packed
    1¼ c. chopped pecans or walnuts
    ½   tsp. salt
    ½   tsp. baking soda
    ¾   c. butter, room temperature

Ingredients for filling:

    1   can pumpkin purée (16 oz.)
    ⅔ c. milk
    ⅓ c. light brown sugar, firmly packed
    1   egg
    1   Tbs. pumpkin pie spice (recipe page 181)

Directions for crust and topping:

1. Preheat oven to 375 degrees F.
2. Combine oats, flour, brown sugar, pecans, salt, soda, and butter; mix until crumbly.
3. Reserve about 1½ cups crumb mixture; press remaining mixture into lightly buttered 13 x 9 x 2-inch baking pan, and bake for 10 minutes.

Directions for filling:

1. While crust is baking, beat filling ingredients until well blended and smooth.
2. Spread filling over crust; sprinkle with reserved crumb mixture.
3. Return to oven and bake 25 minutes longer.
4. Cool and cut into bars.

Yields: 18 to 24 servings.

Soft Spice Bars

These bars have the old-fashioned taste of gingersnaps, but they are chewy and quick to bake.

Ingredients:

¾ c. butter, melted
1 c. plus 2 Tbs. sugar, divided
⅓ c. molasses
1 egg
2 c. all-purpose flour
2 tsp. baking soda
1 tsp. ground cinnamon
½ tsp. ground cloves
½ tsp. ground ginger
¼ tsp. salt

Directions:

1. Preheat oven to 375 degrees F.
2. In mixing bowl combine butter, 1 cup sugar, and molasses.
3. Beat in egg until smooth.
4. Combine flour, baking soda, cinnamon, cloves, ginger, and salt; stir into molasses mixture.
5. Spread into greased 15 x 10 x 1-inch baking pan.
6. Sprinkle with remaining sugar.
7. Bake for 10 to 12 minutes or until lightly browned. (Do not overbake.)
8. Cool on wire rack before cutting.

Yields: 2½ dozen bars.

Did You Know? . . . .

Did you know that in 2006 the two turkeys pardoned by the President were named Flyer and Fryer?

Sour Cream Cranberry Bars

If you love cranberries, you will enjoy these bars.

Ingredients:

- 1 c. butter, softened
- 1 c. brown sugar, firmly packed
- 2 c. quick-cooking oats
- 1½ c. plus 2 Tbs. all-purpose flour, divided
- 2½ c. dried cranberries
- 1 c. sour cream (8 oz.)
- ¾ c. sugar
- 1 egg, lightly beaten
- 1 Tbs. grated lemon peel
- 1 tsp. vanilla extract

Directions:

1. Preheat oven to 350 degrees F.
2. In large mixing bowl cream butter and brown sugar.
3. Combine oats and 1½ cups flour; add to creamed mixture until blended.
4. Set aside 1½ cups for topping.
5. Press remaining crumb mixture into ungreased 13 x 9 x 2-inch baking pan.
6. Bake for 10 to 12 minutes or until lightly browned.
7. Meanwhile, in large bowl combine cranberries, sour cream, sugar, egg, lemon peel, vanilla, and remaining flour.
8. Spread evenly over crust.
9. Sprinkle with reserved crumb mixture.
10. Bake for 20 to 25 minutes or until lightly browned.
11. Cool on wire rack.
12. Refrigerate leftovers.

Yields: About 3 dozen.

Pumpkin Spritz Cookies

I always liked to make spritz cookies with my mom while growing up, and this is a nice variation.

Ingredients:

    1   c. butter, softened
    ½   c. sugar
    ¾   tsp. baking powder
    ¾   tsp. ground cinnamon
    ½   tsp. ground nutmeg
    ¼   tsp. ground ginger
    ⅓   c. pumpkin purée
    1   egg
    1   tsp. vanilla extract
    2¾ c. all-purpose flour
         ground nutmeg

Directions:

1. Preheat oven to 400 degrees F.
2. Cream butter.
3. Add sugar, baking powder, and spices; beat until combined.
4. Beat in pumpkin, egg, and vanilla until combined.
5. Beat in flour.
6. Do not chill.
7. Form with cookie press and sprinkle nutmeg on top.
8. Bake for 6 to 8 minutes.
9. Remove to rack to cool.

Did You Know? . . . .

Did you know that the world's biggest pumpkin pie weighed 418 pounds?

Thanksgiving Delights Cookbook

A Collection of Thanksgiving Recipes
Cookbook Delights Holiday Series Book 11

Desserts

Table of Contents

Page

Did You Know? . . . .

Did you know that when referring to balloons in parades, a falloon is a float-based balloon and a balloonicle is a self-powered balloon vehicle?

Baked Cranberry Pudding

This is an old-fashioned pudding that is a cranberry-lover's delight. Serve warm in crystal serving pieces, topped with whipped cream for an elegant look. You can also serve in bowls with rich cream poured over for a homey touch.

Ingredients for pudding:

1	c. brown sugar, firmly packed
3	eggs, separated
⅔	c. whipping cream
2	tsp. vanilla extract
1	tsp. ground cinnamon
½	tsp. ground nutmeg
1½	c. all-purpose flour
3	Tbs. grated orange peel
1	tsp. baking powder
½	tsp. cream of tartar, divided
⅛	tsp. salt
3½	c. coarsely chopped fresh cranberries
¼	c. butter, melted

Ingredients for topping:

1½	c. sugar
½	c. orange juice
3	c. whole cranberries

Directions for pudding:

1. Preheat oven to 350 degrees F.
2. In bowl combine brown sugar and egg yolks.
3. Add whipping cream, vanilla, cinnamon, and nutmeg; set aside.
4. In large bowl combine flour, orange peel, baking powder, ¼ teaspoon cream of tartar, and salt.

5. Add chopped cranberries; stir to completely coat.
6. Add brown sugar mixture and butter; mix well. (Batter will be stiff.)
7. Beat egg whites until foamy.
8. Add remaining cream of tartar; beat until soft peaks form.
9. Fold into batter.
10. Pour into greased 9-inch springform pan.
11. Bake for 45 to 50 minutes or until wooden pick inserted near center comes out clean.

Directions for topping:

1. While pudding is baking, bring sugar and orange juice to a boil in saucepan.
2. Cook for 3 minutes or until sugar dissolves.
3. Reduce heat; add cranberries and simmer 6 to 8 minutes or until berries begin to burst.
4. Remove from heat and cover.
5. When pudding tests done, place springform pan on jellyroll pan.
6. Spoon warm cranberry sauce over top.
7. Return to oven for 10 minutes.
8. Cool for 10 minutes before removing sides of springform pan.
9. Cool at least 1 hour or overnight.
10. Before serving, reheat at 350 degrees F. for 10 minutes.

Yields: 8 servings.

Did You Know? . . . .

Did you know that Tisquantum (Squanto) was kidnapped and taken to England, where he lived for nine years? He returned to the New World in 1913 with John Smith.

Cranberry Bread Pudding

This makes a colorful Thanksgiving dessert.

Ingredients for pudding:

15 eggs
2½ c. milk
¾ c. brown sugar, firmly packed
2½ tsp. vanilla extract
2½ tsp. ground cinnamon
1 tsp. salt
1½ loaves white bread, cut into 1-inch cubes (about 15 cups)
3 Tbs. unsalted butter, room temperature
2¾ c. dried cranberries
    gingery orange syrup (recipe below)

Ingredients for gingery orange syrup:

2 c. fresh-squeezed orange juice (about 6 oranges)
1 c. corn syrup
⅛ tsp. salt
1 Tbs. fresh-squeezed lemon juice
1 Tbs. finely minced fresh gingerroot
1 Tbs. finely grated orange zest
4 Tbs. unsalted butter, room temperature

Directions for pudding:

1. In large mixing bowl lightly beat together eggs, milk, brown sugar, vanilla, cinnamon, and salt until combined.
2. Add bread cubes, cover with plastic wrap, and soak in refrigerator at least 30 minutes or overnight.
3. Preheat oven to 350 degrees F.
4. Spread butter on all sides of 10-cup fluted baking pan.

5. Sprinkle ¼ cup dried cranberries into baking pan.
6. Stir remaining cranberries into bread cube mixture, and pour mixture into baking pan.
7. Bake until top is golden and firm to touch, about 50 to 60 minutes.
8. Unmold bread pudding, transfer to serving platter, and drizzle with gingery orange syrup.
9. Serve with a dollop of butter.

Directions for gingery orange syrup:

1. In small heavy saucepan combine orange juice and corn syrup over medium heat, stirring occasionally until corn syrup is dissolved.
2. Bring to low boil and cook until thick and syrupy, about 15 minutes.
3. Stir in salt, lemon juice, ginger, and orange zest.
4. Gently whisk in butter.
5. Serve warm.
6. Keep tightly covered in refrigerator for up to 1 week.

Sweetened Whipped Cream

This is a delicious topping on many desserts. Enjoy.

Ingredients:

1   c. heavy cream
¼   c. sugar
1   tsp. vanilla extract

Directions:

1. Whip cream until almost stiff.
2. Add sugar and vanilla; beat until cream holds peaks.

Double-Layer Pumpkin Cheesecake

This is a great alternative to pumpkin pie, especially for cheesecake fans.

Ingredients:

1   graham cracker crust (recipe page 225)
2   pkg. cream cheese (8 oz. each), softened
½   c. sugar
½   tsp. vanilla extract
2   eggs
½   c. pumpkin purée
½   tsp. ground cinnamon
1   pinch ground cloves
1   pinch ground nutmeg
½   c. Sweetened Whipped Cream (recipe page 157)

Directions:

1. Prepare 9-inch graham cracker crust; cool.
2. Preheat oven to 325 degrees F.
3. In large bowl combine cream cheese, sugar, and vanilla; beat until smooth.
4. Blend in eggs one at a time.
5. Remove 1 cup of batter and spread into bottom of crust; set aside.
6. Add pumpkin, cinnamon, cloves, and nutmeg to remaining batter; stir gently until well blended.
7. Carefully spread over batter in crust.
8. Bake for 35 to 40 minutes or until center is almost set.
9. Allow to cool, then refrigerate for 3 hours or overnight.
10. Cover with whipped cream before serving.

Yields: 8 servings.

Apple, Cranberry, and Pear Crisp

This is a variation of the traditional apple crisp. Cranberries can be substituted with raisins or dried cherries. Comice pears taste best with this recipe, so request these from your favorite farmers' market or grocery store.

Ingredients for filling:

    2-3 Rome Beauty apples, peeled, cored, cubed
    2-3 Comice pears, peeled, cored, cubed
    ½   c. dried cranberries
    1   Tbs. all-purpose flour
    2   Tbs. honey
    1½ Tbs. lemon juice

Ingredients for topping:

    ½ c. all-purpose flour
    ½ c. brown sugar, firmly packed
    ⅔ c. oatmeal
    ¾ c. ground walnuts
    ⅔ c. butter

Directions for filling:

    1. Preheat oven to 375 degrees F.
    2. Lightly grease 8-inch square baking dish.
    3. Mix apples, pears, cranberries, flour, honey, and
       lemon juice in prepared dish.

Directions for topping:

    1. In bowl mix all topping ingredients to consistency of
       coarse crumbs.
    2. Sprinkle loosely over fruit mixture.
    3. Bake 45 minutes or until brown and crisp on top.

Yields: 8 servings.

Marbled Pumpkin Cheesecake

The marbling makes this an elegant cheesecake.

Ingredients for crust:

- 1¼ c. graham cracker crumbs
- 2 Tbs. sugar
- ¼ c. butter, melted
- 1 c. semisweet chocolate mini-morsels

Ingredients for filling:

- 1 c. semisweet chocolate mini-morsels
- 24 oz. cream cheese, softened
- 1 c. sugar
- ¼ c. light brown sugar, firmly packed
- 1 can pumpkin purée (16 oz.)
- 4 eggs
- ½ c. evaporated milk
- ¼ c. cornstarch
- ¾ tsp. ground cinnamon
- ⅛ tsp. ground nutmeg

Directions for crust:

1. In medium bowl combine graham cracker crumbs, sugar, and butter.
2. Press onto bottom of greased 10-inch springform pan.
3. Sprinkle with chocolate morsels.

Directions for filling:

1. Preheat oven to 325 degrees F.
2. In small, heavy saucepan over low heat, melt chocolate morsels, stirring constantly until smooth.
3. In large mixing bowl beat cream cheese and sugars.
4. Beat in pumpkin.
5. Beat in eggs and evaporated milk.
6. Beat in cornstarch, cinnamon, and nutmeg.

7. Remove 1 cup pumpkin batter; stir into melted chocolate.
8. Pour remainder of pumpkin batter into springform pan.
9. Pour chocolate mixture over top; swirl.
10. Bake for 60 minutes or until edge of filling is set.
11. Turn oven off; allow cheesecake to stand in oven for 30 minutes.
12. Remove from oven; cool completely.
13. Cover; chill for several hours before serving.

Yields: 12 servings.

Pumpkin Custard

Our family loves custard, and this is full of pumpkin flavor.

Ingredients:

1	c. pumpkin purée
3	eggs
1½	c. milk
⅓	c. sugar
½	tsp. ground cinnamon
¼	tsp. ground cloves
¼	tsp. ground nutmeg
¼	tsp. ground ginger

Directions:

1. Preheat oven to 350 degrees F.
2. Beat all ingredients together.
3. Pour into baking dish.
4. Sprinkle with nutmeg.
5. Bake for about 50 minutes or until custard is set in the middle.

Yields: 4 servings.

Pumpkin Parfait

These pumpkin parfaits can be made ahead for a lighter, chilled dessert.

Ingredients:

- 1   c. mashed, cooked pumpkin
- 1   pt. vanilla ice cream, softened
- ½   c. light brown sugar, firmly packed
- 1   tsp. ground cinnamon
- ½   tsp. ground nutmeg
- ¼   tsp. ground allspice
- ½   c. cold water
- 3   tsp. unflavored gelatin
- ½   c. boiling water
-     Sweetened Whipped Cream (recipe page 157)

Directions:

1. Mix together pumpkin and ice cream; refrigerate.
2. Combine brown sugar, cinnamon, nutmeg, and allspice; mix well and set aside.
3. Dissolve gelatin in cold water; once dissolved, add to sugar mixture while stirring constantly.
4. Add boiling water; stir until dissolved.
5. As soon as all is dissolved, gradually add pumpkin and ice cream mixture; beat well.
6. Spoon into parfait glasses and chill.
7. Top with whipped cream and serve.

Did You Know? . . . .

Did you know that Massachusetts is the second largest U.S. producer of cranberries, with over one-third of total domestic production?

Sweet Potato-Eggnog Casserole Dessert

Eggnog adds a holiday touch to this sweet potato dish.

Ingredients:

    5   lb. sweet potatoes
    ½   c. golden raisins
    ¼   c. brandy
    ⅔   c. eggnog
    3   Tbs. butter, melted
    2   Tbs. sugar
    ⅛   tsp. salt
    2   oatmeal cookies, crushed
    2   Tbs. dark brown sugar, firmly packed
    2   Tbs. chopped pecans, toasted

Directions:

1. Cook sweet potatoes in water to cover in large Dutch oven for 40 minutes or until tender; drain.
2. Cool to touch then peel sweet potatoes and mash.
3. Combine raisins and brandy; let stand 30 minutes; drain.
4. Preheat oven to 350 degrees F.
5. Combine mashed sweet potatoes, eggnog, butter, sugar, and salt; reserve 2 cups sweet potato mixture.
6. Stir raisins into remaining sweet potato mixture; spoon into lightly greased 2-quart baking dish.
7. Combine cookie crumbs, brown sugar, and chopped pecans; sprinkle cookie mixture over top of casserole.
8. Pipe dollops of reserved 2 cups sweet potato mixture around edge of casserole.
9. Bake for 20 minutes or until thoroughly heated.

Yields: 8 servings.

Sweet Potato Flan

Sweet potatoes are easy to mash when baked the day before and placed in the refrigerator until ready to use. Crisp cookies or shortbread go well with this flan.

Ingredients:

- 2 med. sweet potatoes
- ¾ c. sugar
- 2 cans sweetened condensed milk (14 oz. each)
- 2 c. milk
- 10 lg. eggs
- 1 tsp. ground cinnamon
- ½ tsp. ground allspice
- ¼ tsp. ground cloves
- 1 tsp. vanilla extract

Directions:

1. Bake sweet potatoes at 400 degrees F. for 1 hour or until tender; cool to touch.
2. Peel and mash; reserve 1 cup mashed sweet potato.
3. Reduce oven temperature to 325 degrees F.
4. Sprinkle sugar in 10-inch round cake pan.
5. Place over medium heat and cook, shaking pan constantly, until sugar melts and turns light golden brown.
6. Remove from heat; set aside. (Mixture may crack slightly as it cools.)
7. Process ½ cup sweet potato, 1 can condensed milk, and half of next 6 ingredients in blender or food processor until smooth, stopping to scrape down sides; pour into large bowl.
8. Repeat procedure; whisk until combined.
9. Pour mixture over caramelized sugar; cover with aluminum foil and place in large shallow pan.
10. Pour hot water into larger pan to a depth of ½ inch.

11. Bake for 70 to 75 minutes or until knife inserted in center comes out clean.
12. Remove pan from water and uncover.
13. Run knife around edge of pan to loosen and prevent flan from cracking.
14. Cool on wire rack 30 minutes; cover and chill at least 8 hours.
15. Run knife around edge of flan again to loosen; invert onto serving plate.

Yields: 1 (10-inch) flan.

Refreshing Orange Ice

This sherbet can be eaten along with the meal or for a light dessert. Its tangy, creamy flavor complements the turkey and trimmings.

Ingredients:

3   c. water, divided
1   c. sugar
1   can frozen orange juice concentrate (12 oz.), thawed
2   Tbs. lemon juice
½   c. half-and-half

Directions:

1. In saucepan bring 1 cup water and sugar to a boil, stirring frequently.
2. Boil for 1 minute or until sugar is dissolved.
3. Remove from heat; stir in orange juice concentrate, lemon juice, and remaining water.
4. Transfer to freezer-safe mixing bowl.
5. Cover and freeze until firm.
6. Remove from freezer.
7. Beat until blended then beat in half-and-half.
8. Cover and return to freezer.
9. Remove from freezer 20 minutes before serving.

Indian Pudding

We like to honor America's cultural heritage with this Native American pudding.

Ingredients:

    4½ c. milk, divided
    ¼ c. heavy cream
    ¾ c. cornmeal
    ⅓ c. butter
    ½ c. dark molasses
    1 tsp. salt
    ¼ c. sugar
    1 tsp. ground cinnamon

Directions:

1. Preheat oven to 375 degrees F.
2. Grease 1½-quart baking dish.
3. Scald 3½ cups milk in top of double boiler over direct heat.
4. Remove milk from heat.
5. Mix cornmeal with cream and remaining 1 cup milk.
6. Stir this mixture into scalding milk, stirring constantly.
7. Place milk mixture into top of double boiler and cook for 20 minutes, stirring frequently.
8. Stir butter, molasses, salt, sugar, and cinnamon into mixture.
9. Pour into prepared baking dish.
10. Bake for 1½ hours.

Yields: 6 to 8 servings.

Thanksgiving Delights Cookbook

A Collection of Thanksgiving Recipes
Cookbook Delights Holiday Series Book 11

Dressings, Sauces, and Condiments

Table of Contents

Balsamic Vinaigrette

This is a tangy vinaigrette that is wonderful on mixed greens, tomato, onion, and cucumber salads. It is also good if used sparingly over steamed vegetables or stir-fry.

Ingredients:

- ½   c. extra-virgin olive oil
- ½   c. white balsamic vinegar
- 1   clove garlic, crushed
- 1   tsp. ground mustard
- 1   pinch salt
   freshly ground black pepper to taste

Directions:

1. In small bowl whisk together olive oil, vinegar, garlic, and mustard.
2. Season to taste with salt and black pepper.

Yields: About 1 cup.

Cranberry Tomato Chutney

Our family has learned to appreciate chutney with the arrival of our daughter from Bombay, India. The unique flavor of this chutney complements turkey, pork, and duck. To make a quick appetizer, blend up 1½ cups, pour over cream cheese, and serve with crackers.

Ingredients:

- 5   c. cranberries, fresh or frozen
- 1   can crushed tomatoes (28 oz.)
- 1   c. golden raisins
- ¾   c. sugar

1   tsp. salt
¾   tsp. ground ginger

Directions:

1. In large saucepan combine all ingredients.
2. Bring to a boil.
3. Reduce heat, cover, and simmer for 20 to 25 minutes or until cranberries and raisins are tender, stirring occasionally.
4. Cool.
5. Cover and refrigerate for 2 to 3 days before serving.

Yields: 6 cups.

Cinnamon Apple Rings

These apple rings are easy to make and make a great condiment or dessert. They are also good served warm over ice cream.

Ingredients:

½   c. red cinnamon candies
¼   c. sugar
2   c. water
3   med. apples (1 lb.)

Directions:

1. In skillet combine cinnamon candies, sugar, and 2 cups water.
2. Stir over medium heat until sugar and candies are dissolved.
3. Core apples and cut crossways into ½-inch rings.
4. Add rings to syrup.
5. Simmer gently until transparent but not soft.
6. Cool rings in syrup.

Clarified Butter

Use this method to clarify butter for any recipes that call for it.

Directions:

1. Gently melt unsalted butter over low heat until butter breaks down and 3 layers form: top layer–white foam or froth (whey proteins); middle layer–pure golden-yellow liquid called clarified butter; bottom layer–milky layer of solids called milk solids.
2. Skim off top foam layer with spoon.
3. When all white foam is skimmed off surface of clarified butter and it has stopped bubbling, remove saucepan from heat.
4. Let butter sit a few minutes to allow milk solids to further settle to bottom.
5. Strain mixture through fine sieve or cheesecloth-lined strainer. (Liquid collected is the clarified butter.)
6. May be stored, covered, in refrigerator for several months. (Chilled clarified butter does become grainy.)
7. Note: The intensity of flavor of clarified butter depends on how long it is cooked. If you continue to cook the butter once it has melted and separated, milk solids at bottom of pan will start to brown. Once milk solids turn a golden brown color, the clarified butter will take on a rich, fragrant, nutty flavor. Be careful not to overheat butter or it will become bitter tasting.

Did You Know? . . . .

Did you know there are seven major varieties of sweet potatoes?

Cranberry Compote

This cranberry compote is a perfect accompaniment for turkey for your Thanksgiving dinner, but it is also great any time of year with chicken or turkey. You can also use it as a spread on a turkey or chicken sandwich.

Ingredients:

1   bag fresh cranberries (12 oz.), rinsed, picked over
¾   c. sugar
1½   c. water
½   tsp. vanilla extract
1   pinch of salt
⅛   tsp. ground cinnamon
2   Tbs. cornstarch
¾   c. fresh orange juice
     strips of zest from 1 orange (about 2 Tbs.)

Directions:

1. Put cranberries in medium-size nonreactive, nonstick saucepan; add zest.
2. Peel and seed orange, discard white pith, and coarsely chop.
3. Add chopped orange to pot of cranberries along with sugar, water, vanilla, salt, and cinnamon.
4. Bring to a boil over medium heat.
5. Reduce heat to medium-low and simmer for 10 minutes.
6. Dissolve cornstarch in orange juice.
7. Add mixture to cranberries and stir to blend.
8. Simmer another 20 minutes until mixture is thick like syrup.
9. Cool completely then serve with turkey.
10. Compote will keep for 3 days in refrigerator.

Yields: 6 servings.

Cranberry Relish

This is such a simple, flavorful relish, and it is easy to make ahead.

Ingredients:

   2   c. fresh cranberries
   ½   c. sugar
   3   Tbs. lemon juice

Directions:

   1. In small saucepan combine all ingredients.
   2. Bring to a boil then lower to simmer.
   3. Continue to cook until mixture is thick and berries are glazed.
   4. Allow to cool.
   5. Transfer to covered container and refrigerate until needed.

Cranberry Pear Relish

Tart and tempting, this relish is pleasant with both poultry and pork.

Ingredients:

   1   med. navel orange
   4   med. pears, peeled, coarsely chopped
   1   pkg. cranberries, fresh or frozen (12 oz.)
   1   c. brown sugar, firmly packed
   1   tsp. grated orange peel
   ½   tsp. ground cinnamon
   ¼   tsp. ground ginger (or 1 tsp. minced fresh gingerroot)
   ⅛   tsp. ground allspice

Directions:

1. Squeeze juice from orange; add enough water to measure ½ cup.
2. Pour into saucepan; add remaining ingredients.
3. Bring to a boil; reduce heat.
4. Simmer uncovered for 25 to 30 minutes or until cranberries pop and mixture is thickened.
5. Cool.
6. Cover and store in refrigerator.

Yields: 4 cups.

Blue Cheese Dressing

Blue cheese dressing is great with vegetables, crackers, and breads.

Ingredients:

¼ c. onion, finely chopped
1 c. mayonnaise
¼ tsp. celery seed
1 dash pepper
½ tsp. salt
½ tsp. paprika
1 c. crumbled blue cheese

Directions:

1. Put all ingredients except cheese in blender.
2. Cover; blend until smooth.
3. Remove dressing from blender; stir in blue cheese.
4. Cover and chill.

Yields: 2½ cups.

Cranberry Salad Dressing

This is a tangy salad dressing.

Ingredients:

- 1 c. fresh cranberries
- 1 med. navel orange, peeled, sectioned
- ⅔ c. sugar
- ½ c. vinegar
- 1 tsp. salt
- 1 tsp. ground mustard
- 1 tsp. grated onion
- 1 c. vegetable oil

Directions:

1. In blender combine cranberries, orange sections, sugar, vinegar, salt, ground mustard, and onion; blend well.
2. While blending, remove cover and gradually add oil in steady stream.
3. Store in covered container in refrigerator.

Yields: 2½ cups.

Fresh Cranberry Orange Relish

My dad used to love this simple cranberry relish.

Ingredients:

- 1   med. to lg. orange
- 12 oz. cranberries, fresh or frozen
- ¾-1 c. sugar (to your personal taste)

Directions:

1. Slice unpeeled orange into eighths; remove seeds.
2. Place half the cranberries and half the orange slices in food processor container.
3. Process until mixture is evenly chopped; transfer to bowl.
4. Repeat with remaining cranberries and orange slices.
5. Stir in sugar to desired sweetness.
6. Store in refrigerator or freezer.
7. Note: May also be prepared in food grinder.

Yields: About 2½ cups.

Savory Turkey Gravy

This simple, rich gravy is delicious over mashed potatoes.

Ingredients:

5   c. turkey stock
1   c. water
¼   c. all-purpose flour
1   tsp. poultry seasoning (recipe page 178)
½   tsp. ground black pepper
¼   tsp. celery salt
1   tsp. salt

Directions:

1. In medium saucepan bring turkey stock to a boil.
2. Gradually dissolve flour in water.
3. Slowly stir flour mixture into turkey stock.
4. Stir in seasonings.
5. Boil to desired consistency.

Yields: 4 cups.

Italian Vinaigrette Dressing

This is a simple dressing that is full of flavor. Adjust the seasonings to your own personal taste.

Ingredients:

- ¼ c. olive oil
- ¼ c. water
- ⅓ c. white vinegar
- 3 Tbs. grated Parmesan cheese
- ½ tsp. dried oregano
- ½ tsp. dried sage
- ½ tsp. dried basil
- ½ tsp. paprika
- ¼ tsp. dry mustard
- ¼ tsp. black pepper
- 1 clove garlic, crushed

Directions:

1. Combine all ingredients in screw-top jar.
2. Cover and shake well.
3. Store in refrigerator up to 2 weeks.

Yields: About ¾ cup.

Mixed Fruit Cranberry Relish

This makes a pleasant autumn relish.

Ingredients:

- 12 oz. fresh cranberries
- 1 c. raisins
- ½ c. golden raisins

½ c. roasted pecan pieces
3 firm apples, quartered, seeded
24 pitted dates, cut in half
3 Tbs. pure maple syrup
2 Tbs. kosher brandy
2 sliced persimmons

Directions:

1. In food processor put cranberries, raisins, golden raisins, pecans, apples, and dates; pulse until finely chopped.
2. Transfer to medium bowl.
3. Stir in maple syrup and brandy until thoroughly combined. (Mixture will be very moist.)
4. Transfer mixture to clear glass serving bowl.
5. Garnish by lining sides of bowl with sliced persimmons.

Italian Seasoning Mix

This is a great combination of spices to use whenever you need some Italian spice.

Ingredients:

6 Tbs. dried basil
1 Tbs. dried marjoram
2 Tbs. dried oregano
1 Tbs. dried thyme

Directions:

1. Mix all ingredients together thoroughly.
2. Store in airtight container.

Poultry Seasoning

Besides poultry, season a variety of foods such as dressing, stuffing, and even meatloaf with this spice mixture.

Ingredients:

- 1 Tbs. dried rosemary
- 1 Tbs. dried sage
- 1 Tbs. dried thyme
- 1 Tbs. dried marjoram
- 1 Tbs. celery seed
- ¾ tsp. freshly ground black pepper

Directions:

1. Grind ingredients together in spice grinder, mini food processor, or mortar and pestle.
2. Store in airtight container.

Yields: About ⅓ cup.

Giblet Gravy

This old-fashioned giblet gravy recipe is very easy to prepare.

Ingredients:

- 3 Tbs. turkey drippings
- 3 Tbs. all-purpose flour
- 2½ c. turkey stock
- ¼ c. cooked turkey giblets, chopped
- 1½ tsp. chopped fresh sage
- ½ tsp. ground black pepper
  salt to taste

Directions:

1. Heat pan drippings in large skillet over medium heat.
2. Gradually add flour and stir until golden brown.
3. Slowly whisk in turkey stock until blended and smooth.
4. Stir in giblets.
5. Season with sage, pepper, and salt.
6. Bring to a boil, reduce heat, and simmer for 8 to 10 minutes or until thickened.

Yields: 6 to 8 servings.

Whole-Berry Cranberry Sauce

Some of the family prefer whole berries to jellied cranberry sauce.

Ingredients:

1   c. sugar
1   c. water
12 oz. cranberries, fresh or frozen

Directions:

1. Mix sugar and water in medium saucepan; stir to dissolve sugar.
2. Bring to a boil; add cranberries
3. Return to a boil; reduce heat.
4. Boil gently 10 minutes, stirring occasionally.
5. Remove from heat.
6. Cool completely at room temperature then refrigerate.

Yields: About 2¼ cups.

Seasoned Salt

This is a great seasoned salt to use on many things. You can also package it in decorative jars for gifts.

Ingredients:

- 1   c. salt
- 2   tsp. sugar
- 2   tsp. dry mustard
- 1½ tsp. dried oregano
- 1½ tsp. garlic powder
- 1   tsp. curry powder
- 1   tsp. onion powder
- ½   tsp. celery seeds
- ¼   tsp. paprika
- ¼   tsp. ground thyme
- ⅛   tsp. ground turmeric

Directions:

1. Combine all ingredients; shake to blend.
2. Store in airtight container.

Yields: 1⅓ cups.

Jellied Cranberry Sauce

Some of the family love jellied cranberry sauce instead of the whole-berry version, so we make and serve both.

Ingredients:

- 1   c. sugar
- 1   c. water
- 12 oz. cranberries, fresh or frozen

Directions:

1. Mix sugar and water in medium saucepan; stir to dissolve sugar.
2. Bring to a boil; add cranberries.
3. Return to a boil; reduce heat.
4. Boil gently 10 minutes, stirring occasionally.
5. Remove from heat.
6. Place wire mesh strainer over mixing bowl.
7. Pour contents of saucepan into strainer.
8. Mash cranberries with back of spoon, frequently scraping outside of strainer, until no pulp is left.
9. Stir contents of bowl; pour into serving container.
10. Cover and cool completely at room temperature.
11. Refrigerate until serving time.

Yields: About 1 cup.

Pumpkin Pie Spice

This makes a great spice to have around, and it also makes an appreciated gift when packaged in small decorative jars.

Ingredients:

2 Tbs. ground cinnamon
1 Tbs. ground ginger
1½ tsp. ground allspice
1½ tsp. ground cloves

Directions:

1. Mix all ingredients together thoroughly.
2. Store in airtight container.

Yields: ¼ cup.

Vegetarian Gravy

I have two vegetarian daughters, and they enjoy a flavorful gravy. Adjust the seasonings as you like them.

Ingredients:

- ½ c. butter
- ½ c. minced onion
- 4 cloves garlic, minced
- ¼ Tbs. all-purpose flour
- 4 c. vegetable stock
- 5 Tbs. soy sauce
- 2 Tbs. minced fresh parsley
- 2 Tbs. chopped chives
- ½ tsp. dried sage
- ½ tsp. dried thyme
- ½ tsp. dried rosemary
- 1 c. half-and-half (optional)
   pepper to taste

Directions:

1. In heavy skillet sauté onion and garlic in butter about 2 minutes.
2. Transfer to bowl and wipe skillet clean.
3. Add flour to skillet and cook, stirring constantly until flour is brown and toasted.
4. Add stock and soy sauce; cook, whisking constantly until mixture comes to a boil and thickens, about 5 minutes.
5. Stir in onion/garlic mixture and seasonings.
6. Cook for 1 minute more.
7. If gravy becomes too thick, thin with additional stock.
8. If you like a creamy gravy, add 1 cup half-and-half at the end, but do not boil.

Yields: About 4½ cups.

Thanksgiving Delights Cookbook

A Collection of Thanksgiving Recipes
Cookbook Delights Holiday Series Book 11

Jams, Jellies, and Syrups

Table of Contents

Page

Did You Know? . . . .

Did you know that the largest balloon to be in the Macy's parade was Superman?

A Basic Guide for Canning Jams, Jellies, and Syrups

1. Wash jars in hot, soapy water inside and out with brush or soft cloth.
2. Run your finger around rim of each jar, discarding any with cracks or chips.
3. Rinse well in clean, clear, hot water, using tongs to avoid burns to hands or fingers.
4. Place upside down on clean cloth to drain well.
5. Place lids in boiling water for 2 minutes to sterilize and keep hot until placing on rim of jar.
6. Immediately prior to filling each jar, immerse in very hot water with tongs to heat jar (avoids breakage of jar with hot liquid).
7. Fill jar to within 1 inch of top of rim or to level recommended in recipe.
8. Wipe rim with clean damp cloth to remove any particles of food, and check again for any chips or cracks.
9. With tongs, place lid from hot bath directly onto rim of jar.
10. Using gloves, cloth, or holders, tighten lid firmly onto jar with ring or use single formed lid in place of ring to cover inner lid. Do not tighten down too hard as it may impede sealing.
11. Place on protected surface to cool, taking care to not disturb lid and ring. A slight indentation of lid will be apparent when sealed.
12. Leave overnight until thoroughly cooled.
13. When cooled, wipe jars with damp cloth and then label and date each.
14. Store upright on shelf in cool, dark place.

Apple Butter

One of our family favorites is homemade apple butter. Make extra because it disappears quickly. It also makes great gifts.

Ingredients:

    15 med. firm, tart cooking apples (4 to 5 lb.)
    1½ qt. cider
    3   c. sugar
    1   tsp. ground cinnamon
    1   tsp. ground allspice
    1   tsp. ground cloves
    ¼   tsp. ground nutmeg

Directions:

1. Wash and slice apples; do not remove core, seeds, or peel.
2. Place apples in large saucepan; add cider and boil 15 minutes or until soft.
3. Press through sieve (you should have about 3 quarts of pulp).
4. Gently boil pulp 1 hour or until it begins to thicken, stirring occasionally.
5. Stir in sugar and spices, and continue cooking slowly 3 hours or until thickened, stirring frequently.
6. Pour into hot sterilized jars, leaving ¼-inch headspace.
7. Process following directions for canning on page 184.

Yields: About 3½ pints.

Apple-Pear Butter

The addition of pears adds flavor to the traditional apple butter.

Ingredients:

    4   lb. tart apples and pears
    2   c. cider, mild cider vinegar, white wine, or water
    ½   c. sugar for each cup of pulp
    2   tsp. ground cinnamon
    1   tsp. ground cloves
    ½   tsp. ground allspice
    1   lemon (grated rind and juice)
        few grains of salt

Directions:

1. Cut apples and pears into pieces (do not core or peel).
2. Cover with cider; cook until soft.
3. Put through sieve.
4. Add remaining ingredients.
5. Cover and cook over low heat until sugar dissolves.
6. Uncover and cook over medium heat until thick and smooth when spooned onto cold plate. (Stir with wooden spoon during cooking.)
7. Ladle into hot jars.
8. Process in hot water bath canner for 10 minutes, following canning directions on page 184.

Yields: About 4 pints.

Did You Know? . . . .

Did you know that turkey is generally considered healthier and less fattening than red meat?

Cranberry Jam

This cranberry jam is very festive.

Ingredients:

7½ c. prepared fruit (2 lb. fully ripe cranberries)
4   c. water
5½ c. sugar
½   tsp. butter
1   pouch liquid fruit pectin

Directions:

1. Wash and sterilize jars and lids.
2. Fill canner half full with water; bring to a simmer.
3. Place cranberries and water in large saucepan.
4. Bring to a boil; reduce heat to low.
5. Cover and simmer 10 minutes.
6. Press through sieve, if desired.
7. Measure exactly 7½ cups prepared fruit into large pan; stir sugar in all at once.
8. Add butter to reduce foaming.
9. Bring mixture to full rolling boil on high heat, stirring constantly; stir in pectin.
10. Return to full rolling boil and boil exactly 1 minute, stirring constantly.
11. Skim off any foam with metal spoon.
12. Ladle quickly into prepared jars, filling to within ⅛ inch of tops.
13. Wipe jar rims and threads.
14. Cover with lids; screw bands tightly.
15. Place jars on elevated rack in canner.
16. Lower rack into canner. (Water must cover jars by 1 to 2 inches. Add boiling water if necessary.)
17. Cover; bring water to gentle boil; process 10 minutes.
18. Remove jars and place upright on towel to cool completely.
19. After jars cool, check seals.

Yields: 10 half-pints.

Cranberry-Orange Marmalade

Oranges add a nice flavor to this cranberry marmalade.

Ingredients:

1   c. sugar
½   c. water
⅛   tsp. ground cloves
1   c. cranberries
3   c. orange marmalade (purchased or use recipe page 192)
⅓   c. orange liqueur or orange juice
3   Tbs. grated orange peel
2   Tbs. brandy (optional)

Directions:

1. Cook sugar, water, and cloves in small, heavy saucepan over low heat, stirring until sugar dissolves.
2. Increase heat and bring to a boil.
3. Add cranberries.
4. Simmer until cranberries are soft but still retain shape, stirring occasionally, about 4 minutes.
5. Cool slightly.
6. Bring marmalade, orange liqueur, orange peel, and brandy to a boil in medium, heavy saucepan.
7. Boil until mixture registers 220 degrees F. (jelly stage) on candy thermometer, stirring occasionally, about 20 minutes.
8. Cool slightly.
9. Using slotted spoon, transfer cranberries from cooking liquid to marmalade (discard liquid).
10. Mix gently.
11. Spoon into jelly jars; seal tightly.
12. Cool completely; refrigerate.
13. Can be prepared 4 weeks ahead.

Yields: 4 half-pints.

Caramel Apple Jam

Try this caramel apple jam.

Ingredients:

   6   c. peeled and diced Granny Smith or Gala apples
   ½   c. water
   ½   tsp. butter
   1   pkg. powdered fruit pectin
   3   c. sugar
   2   c. brown sugar, firmly packed
   ½   tsp. ground cinnamon
   ¼   tsp. ground nutmeg

Directions:

1. In large saucepan mix apples, water, and butter.
2. Cook and stir over low heat until apples are soft but not mushy.
3. Stir in pectin.
4. Bring to a full boil, stirring constantly.
5. Add sugars, cinnamon, and nutmeg.
6. Return to rolling boil and continue to boil, stirring constantly, for 1 minute.
7. Remove from heat; skim foam.
8. Pour into hot jars leaving ¼-inch headspace.
9. Process in boiling water bath for 10 minutes, following canning directions on page 184.

Yields: 7½ pints.

Did You Know? . . . .

Did you know that a female domesticated turkey is called a hen, a chick is called a poult, and in the United States a male is called a tom, but in Europe a male is called a stag?

Honey Pumpkin Butter

This pumpkin butter makes a great gift.

Ingredients:

    2   c. pumpkin purée
    ½   c. honey
    1   tsp. grated lemon rind
    1   Tbs. lemon juice
    1   tsp. ground cinnamon
    ¼   tsp. ground nutmeg
    ¼   tsp. ground ginger
    ⅛   tsp. ground cloves

Directions:

1. Mix all ingredients thoroughly in large saucepan.
2. Simmer uncovered on low heat about 40 minutes, stirring frequently until thick.
3. Ladle into jars and refrigerate.

Yields: 1½ cups.

Pumpkin Preserves

These preserves resemble marmalade both in texture and taste and serve as a wonderful glaze for ham as well as a delightful topping for ice cream.

Ingredients:

    2-3 oranges, thinly sliced
    1-2 lemons, thinly sliced
    12 whole cloves
        desired cups of pumpkin
        sugar (1 cup to every 2 cups pumpkin)

Directions:

1. Peel and cube meat of pumpkin.
2. Measure out 1 cup sugar to every 2 cups pumpkin.
3. Layer in roasting pan along with slices of orange and lemon; allow to sit overnight.
4. Place over medium heat and add cloves.
5. Cook, stirring frequently, until pumpkin is transparent, about 2 hours.
6. Fill jars, seal, and keep refrigerated until used.

Pumpkin-Apple Butter Spread

Try this thick and delicious pumpkin-apple butter the next time you make fresh homemade bread, on biscuits or cornbread, or even on hot cereal.

Ingredients:

1   can pumpkin purée (15 oz.)
1   med. apple, peeled, grated
1   c. apple juice
½   c. brown sugar, firmly packed
¾   tsp. pumpkin pie spice (recipe page 181)

Directions:

1. Combine all ingredients in medium, heavy-duty saucepan.
2. Bring to a boil; reduce heat to low.
3. Cook, stirring occasionally, for 1½ hours.
4. Cool, then store in airtight container in refrigerator for up to 2 months.

Yields: 3 cups.

Orange Marmalade

Orange marmalade is a great flavor addition to your dinner.

Ingredients:

3	c. prepared fruit (about 3 med. oranges and 2 med. lemons)
1½	c. water
⅛	tsp. baking soda
5	c. sugar
½	tsp. butter
1	pouch liquid fruit pectin

Directions:

1. Bring canner, half full with water, to simmer.
2. Wash jars and lids; rinse.
3. Remove colored part of peel from oranges and lemons using vegetable peeler.
4. Cut into thin slivers and finely chop or grind; set aside.
5. Peel and discard remaining white part of peel from fruit.
6. Chop fruit pulp, reserving any juice; set aside.
7. Place peels, water, and baking soda in saucepan.
8. Bring to a boil over high heat.
9. Reduce heat; cover and simmer 20 minutes, stirring occasionally.
10. Add reserved fruit and juice; cover.
11. Simmer an additional 10 minutes.
12. Measure exactly 3 cups prepared fruit into 6-quart saucepan.
13. Stir sugar into prepared fruit.
14. Add butter to reduce foaming.
15. Bring mixture to full rolling boil over high heat, stirring constantly; stir in pectin.
16. Return to full rolling boil and boil exactly 1 minute, stirring constantly.

17. Remove from heat; skim off any foam with metal spoon.
18. Ladle immediately into prepared jars, filling to within ⅛ inch of tops.
19. Wipe jar rims and threads.
20. Cover with 2-piece lids; screw bands tightly.
21. Place jars on elevated rack in canner.
22. Lower rack into canner. (Water must cover jars by 1 to 2 inches. Add boiling water if necessary.)
23. Cover, bring water to gentle boil, and process 10 minutes.
24. Remove jars and place upright on towel to cool completely.
25. When cool, store in cool, dark place.

Yields: 6 half-pints.

Strawberry-Cranberry Jam

This makes a great holiday jam.

Ingredients:

1½ c. coarsely ground cranberries
2½ c. crushed strawberries, fresh or frozen
2   Tbs. vinegar
4   c. sugar

Directions:

1. Boil berries and vinegar in extra-large kettle for 3 minutes.
2. Add sugar; stir well.
3. Bring to rolling boil and continue boiling 10 to 12 minutes, stirring constantly.
4. Remove from heat and skim.
5. Let stand 24 hours, stirring frequently.
6. Pour cold into sterilized jars and seal.
7. Note: Do not substitute lemon juice for vinegar.

Peach Rum Preserves

Rum adds extra flavor to these peach preserves.

Ingredients:

    4   c. scalded, peeled, finely chopped peaches
    1   env. powdered fruit pectin (1¾   oz.)
    5   c. sugar
    ¼   c. light rum

Directions:

1. Combine peaches and pectin in large saucepan or Dutch oven.
2. Place over high heat and bring to full, rolling boil, stirring constantly.
3. Immediately add all sugar and stir again.
4. Return to full, rolling boil, stirring constantly.
5. Remove from heat; stir in rum.
6. Skim off foam.
7. Continue to stir and skim for 5 minutes to cool mixture slightly and keep fruit well-distributed.
8. Ladle into hot, scalded jars.
9. Seal at once, following canning directions on page 184.

Yields: 6 half-pints.

Did You Know? . . . .

Did you know that turkey droppings are planned to fuel an electric power plant in western Minnesota that will begin operating in 2007? The plant will provide 55 megawatts of power using 700,000 tons of dung per year. Three such plants are in operation in England.

Pear Marmalade

Pears make a nice variation to the usual marmalade.

Ingredients:

- 1½ lb. ripe pears
- 1   orange
- 1   can crushed pineapple (8 oz.)
- 20 maraschino cherries, chopped
- 5   c. sugar
- 1   box powdered pectin

Directions:

1. Peel and core pears.
2. Grind pears and unpeeled orange (or finely chop).
3. Add undrained pineapple.
4. Combine fruits in large saucepan (should have 4½ cups).
5. Add pectin.
6. Place over high heat; stir until mixture comes to a hard boil.
7. Stir in sugar at once.
8. Bring to a boil again and boil hard 1 minute, stirring constantly.
9. Remove from heat, skim off foam, and then stir and skim by turns for 5 minutes.
10. Ladle into jars.
11. When cool, cover with melted paraffin to seal.

Did You Know? . . . .

Did you know that 1941 was the year Congress passed a joint resolution that set Thanksgiving on the fourth Thursday of November, where it remains today?

Pumpkin Butter

This butter also makes a great gift and is delicious on toast and English muffins.

Ingredients:

    3½ c. fresh ground pumpkin or canned pumpkin purée
    2½ c. light brown sugar, firmly packed
    1   lemon, juice and grated rind
    1   Tbs. ground ginger
    1½ tsp. ground cinnamon
    ¼   tsp. ground allspice

Directions:

1. If using fresh pumpkin, mix with sugar, lemon, ginger, cinnamon, and allspice in large bowl.
2. Let stand at room temperature 8 to 10 hours.
3. Transfer to heavy saucepan, add ½ cup water, and bring to a boil.
4. Simmer on low heat, stirring often, for 40 to 60 minutes, to desired consistency.
5. If using canned pumpkin, mix ingredients in heavy saucepan; bring to a boil and simmer on low about 20 minutes to thicken.
6. Pour mixture into hot, sterile, 6-ounce canning jars, leaving ½-inch headspace.
7. Seal with sterile, 2-part lids and rings.
8. Process 10 minutes in boiling water bath, following canning directions on page 184.
9. Cool; adjust seals.

Yields: 5 jars (6 ounces each).

Did You Know? . . . .

Did you know that the average lifespan for a turkey is 10 years?

Thanksgiving Delights Cookbook

A Collection of Thanksgiving Recipes
Cookbook Delights Holiday Series Book 11

Main Dishes

Table of Contents

Turkey Thawing Methods

The experts recommend refrigerator thawing; however, if you are short on time and need a quicker method for thawing, try one of these.

Directions:

1. Thawing turkey at room temperature allows bacterial growth and is not recommended.
2. To thaw a turkey in the refrigerator, thaw breast side up in its unopened wrapper on a tray.
3. Allow at least one day of thawing for every 4 pounds of turkey, and be sure to drain juices off the tray before they overflow.
4. To cold thaw the turkey, thaw breast side down in its unopened wrapper in cold water to cover.
5. Change water every 30 minutes to keep surface cold.
6. Estimate minimum thawing time to be 30 minutes per pound for whole turkey.
7. Neck and giblets in plastic bags allow easy removal.
8. Unique leg tuck eliminates trussing.

Turkey Cooking Methods

There are literally hundreds of ways to cook a turkey, and each year new recipes and techniques are created based on trendy regional ingredients and creative cooking methods. Some are good, some are bad, and some are downright unsafe. All are designed to tantalize the senses and produce the perfect turkey – moist breast meat, tender legs and thighs, golden brown skin, and memorable flavor.

The greatest challenge for new and experienced cooks alike is to avoid the dreaded "dry turkey," which is usually in reference to the white meat of the turkey breast. Because the flavor of turkey marries well with a host of ingredients, turkey can be successfully braised, roasted, grilled, fried, boiled, broiled, barbequed, and so on.

Believe it or not, cooking a turkey is not that difficult. Which turkey cooking method chosen is up to the cook. Just make sure it is a safe method.

Always remember to wash hands, utensils, sink, and anything else that has come in contact with the raw turkey with hot, soapy water immediately following preparation.

Unsafe Turkey Cooking Methods

It is very important to be totally safe while preparing your holiday turkey for your family. Please follow all warnings provided on your turkey label.

Brown Paper Bag Method

This method involves placing the turkey in a large brown paper bag, the type used in grocery stores, and cooking the bird at a very low temperature. Experts agree that brown paper bags were never intended for use as cooking utensils. The glue, ink, chemicals, and other materials used in recycling grocery bags are unsanitary, and some bags may even contain tiny metal shavings.

Make it Safe: To make this method safe, replace the brown bag with a turkey-size oven cooking bag. Cooking turkey at temperatures below 325 degrees F. is unsafe, so increase the oven temperature to 350 degrees F. Use a meat thermometer inserted in the thickest part of the thigh, and cook the turkey until the temperature reaches 165 degrees F.

Trash Bag Method

This method is also known as the "Mississippi Trash Bag Method." A whole turkey is placed in a large trash bag and marinated in salt brine, herbs, and spices for several hours at room temperature. The unsafe part of the method is the use of a trash bag and no refrigeration during marinating. Never use non-food-grade materials as holding vessels for food. Chemicals and non-food colors may leach into the food.

Make it Safe: To make this method safe, replace the trash bag with a large oven-cooking bag. Refrigerate the turkey during the marinating process, and the results will be safe and just as good.

Slow-Cooking Overnight Method

This method is dangerous and involves cooking the turkey at 190 to 200 degrees F. overnight or for 12 to 13 hours. There are many versions of the slow-cooking method around, and all of them put you and your dinner guests at risk of food-borne illness (food poisoning). A low oven temperature means the turkey will take longer to heat, increasing the risk of harmful bacteria growth and the production of toxins that may not be destroyed with further cooking.

Make it Safe: The USDA recommends temperatures no lower than 325 degrees F. for cooking meat and poultry.

Turducken

A turducken is a partially boned turkey layered with a boned duck then with a boned chicken and spread with layers of stuffing between each bird. The entire mass is rolled, tied, and roasted at 190 degrees F. for 12 to 13 hours.

Make it Safe: USDA Hotline representatives recommend keeping the birds chilled until ready to assemble. While boning each bird, keep the others refrigerated. After all three birds have been boned and the stuffing has been prepared, assemble the Turducken ingredients and quickly get it into an oven preheated to 325 degrees F. Use a meat thermometer inserted in the thickest part of the bundle, and cook the turducken to an internal temperature of 165 degrees F. or more. Check the temperature in several locations.

A final note

Please carefully follow the above warnings to keep your family and friends safe from any mishandling.

Traditional Roast Turkey

There is nothing like traditional turkey. It is now recommended <u>not</u> to cook with stuffing inside, so do be careful. Your turkey will be best when cooked with a thermometer so it is done perfectly.

Directions:

1. Preheat oven to 325 degrees F.
2. Check wrapper to see how much turkey weighs and determine approximate cooking time (see chart on page 202).
3. Remove giblet bag from breast and remove neck from turkey cavity.
4. Wash turkey inside and out, and pat skin dry with paper towels.
5. Place turkey breast side up on rack in shallow (about 2 inches deep) roasting pan.
6. Rub turkey with melted butter, onion salt, garlic salt, and pepper.
7. Insert meat thermometer in thigh.
8. Add ½ cup water to bottom of pan, if desired.
9. Cover turkey tightly with tent of heavy-duty aluminum foil or roasting cover.
10. Roast turkey until temperature in thickest part of thigh reaches 165 degrees F. (Cooking time will vary. For example, a 20-pound turkey will take 4¼ to 5 hours to cook; check temperature on thermometer after 4¼ hours.)
11. Meanwhile, mix stuffing or dressing and place in casserole instead of turkey for health safety.
12. Place dressing in oven during last hour or so of roasting time.
13. Remove foil tent after 1 to 1½ hours of cooking time to brown skin.
14. Brush with vegetable oil to enhance browning, if desired.
15. A whole turkey is done when the temperature reaches 165 degrees F.

16. Thigh juices should run clear (not pink) when pierced with a fork, and the leg joint should move freely.
17. Allow turkey to sit 20 to 30 minutes before carving to allow juices to saturate meat evenly.

USDA Roasting Timetable for Unstuffed Fresh or Thawed Turkey at 325 degrees F.

These times are approximate and should always be used in conjunction with a properly placed thermometer.

4 to 8 pounds	1½ to 3¼ hours
8 to 12 pounds	2¾ to 3 hours
12 to 14 pounds	3 to 3¾ hours
14 to 18 pounds	3¾ to 4¼ hours
18 to 20 pounds	4¼ to 4½ hours
20 to 24 pounds	4½ to 5 hours

Microwave Oven Cooked Turkey

Cooking a whole, stuffed turkey in the microwave oven is not recommended. Full-size microwave ovens (650 to 700 watts) can usually accommodate a small turkey (8 to 10 pounds), turkey breast, or boneless turkey roll. Make sure turkey is fully thawed, as microwave thawing followed by microwave cooking creates uneven cooking. This recommendation is very important for health safety.

1. A whole turkey takes 7 to 9 minutes per pound at 50 percent power and rotating the dish every 15 minutes. (Consider using an oven-cooking bag to ensure even cooking.)
2. Turkey roll or boneless turkey breast can be cooked using a microwave probe. (Follow manual directions for monitoring temperature with a probe.)

Deep-Fried Turkey

Deep-fried turkey is very popular in some areas. Try it this year using one of the marinades listed below.

Equipment:

1. A 40- or 60-quart heavy pot with lid and basket.
2. Burner and propane gas tank.
3. Candy thermometer to measure oil temperature.
4. Food thermometer to determine doneness of the turkey.
5. Fire extinguisher.
6. Oven mitts and pot holders.

Location:

1. Place fryer on level dirt or a grassy area.
2. Never fry a turkey indoors, in a garage, or in any other structure attached to a building.
3. Avoid frying on wood decks, which could catch fire, and concrete, which can be stained by the oil.

Ingredients for turkey:

1   turkey (10 to 14 lb.), thawed
5   gal. peanut or canola oil
    marinade (select your favorite from recipes below)

Ingredients for Basic Marinade:

2   cans chicken stock (14 oz. each)
½   c. hot sauce
½   tsp. garlic powder
½   tsp. onion powder

Ingredients for Cajun Marinade:

4   oz. liquid garlic
4   oz. liquid celery
4   oz. liquid onion

1 Tbs. cayenne
2 Tbs. salt
2 Tbs. hot red pepper sauce
1 oz. liquid crab boil

Ingredients for Teriyaki Marinade:

1 c. teriyaki sauce
1 Tbs. garlic powder
1 Tbs. onion powder
1 Tbs. ginger powder

Ingredients for Tasty Marinade:

1 lb. unsalted butter
3 Tbs. salt
3 Tbs. ground black pepper
1 Tbs. ground white pepper
2 Tbs. cayenne pepper

Ingredients for Fresh Garlic-Lemon Marinade:

¾ c. extra-virgin olive oil
¾ c. fresh lemon juice
1 Tbs. zest of lemon
6 lg. cloves garlic
2 tsp. salt
1 tsp. black pepper

Directions for Basic Marinade:

1. Mix ingredients together.
2. Draw marinade into injector.
3. Inject into thickest parts of turkey in about 6 to 10 different places.
4. Put turkey back in refrigerator for 12 to 24 hours.

Directions for Cajun Marinade:

1. Mix ingredients together.
2. Draw marinade into injector.

3. Inject into thickest parts of turkey in about 6 to 10 different places.
4. Put turkey back in refrigerator for 12 to 24 hours.

Directions for Teriyaki Marinade:

1. Mix ingredients together.
2. Draw marinade into injector.
3. Inject into thickest parts of turkey in about 6 to 10 different places.
4. Put turkey back in refrigerator for 12 to 24 hours.

Directions for Tasty Marinade:

1. Melt butter and combine with remaining ingredients.
2. Cool to about 100 degrees F.
3. Inject into turkey just before frying.

Directions for Fresh Garlic-Lemon Marinade:

1. Combine ingredients and purée in blender.
2. Draw marinade into injector.
3. Inject into thickest parts of turkey in about 6 to 10 different places.
4. Put turkey back in refrigerator for 12 to 24 hours.

Directions to prepare turkey:

1. Be sure to measure for oil before breading or marinating turkey.
2. To determine correct amount of oil, place turkey in fryer basket and place in pot.
3. Add water until it reaches 1 to 2 inches above turkey.
4. Remove turkey and note water level, using a ruler to measure distance from top of pot to surface of water.
5. Pour out water and dry pot thoroughly.
6. Add oil to level measured in step 4, and heat oil to 365 to 375 degrees F. (Depending on the amount

of oil used, this usually takes between 45 minutes and 1 hour.)

7. While oil is heating, prepare turkey as desired.
8. If injecting marinade into turkey, purée ingredients so they will pass through the needle. (Even so, mixture may need to be strained to remove larger portions.)
9. Remove any excess fat around neck.
10. If breading turkey, place turkey in gallon-size food-safe storage bag with breading and shake to coat.
11. DO NOT stuff turkeys for deep-frying.
12. To reduce spattering, thoroughly dry interior and exterior of bird.

Directions to fry turkey:

1. Once oil has come to temperature, place turkey in basket and slowly lower into pot.
2. Whole turkeys require about 3 to 3½ minutes per pound to cook.
3. Remove turkey and check internal temperature with meat thermometer—temperature should be at least 165 degrees F. but preferably 170 degrees F. in breast and 165 degrees F. in thigh.
4. Turkey parts such as breast, wings, and thighs require approximately 4 to 5 minutes per pound to come to temperature.
5. Let sit 10 to 20 minutes before carving.

Additional safety tips:

1. Never leave hot oil unattended and do not allow children or pets near cooking area.
2. Never cook turkey with lid on pot because oil temperature will quickly get out of control.
3. Allow oil to cool completely before disposing or storing.
4. Immediately wash hands, utensils, equipment, and surfaces that have come in contact with raw turkey.

5. Turkey should be consumed immediately and leftovers stored in refrigerator within 2 hours of cooking.

Oil selection:

1. Only oils that have high smoke points should be used.
2. Top choice of many cooks is peanut oil.
3. Other oils include canola and sunflower.

Oil Filtering:

1. High smoke-point oils allow reusing the oil with proper filtration.
2. Depending on recipe used, remember to filter oil—not just strain it.
3. Allow oil to cool overnight in covered pot.
4. Strain cooled oil through fine strainer.
5. If breading, spice rub, or herb rub is used in preparation of turkey, oil will need to be further filtered through fine cheesecloth.

Oil storage:

1. Peanut oil should be covered and refrigerated to prevent it from becoming rancid.
2. Peanut oil is more perishable than other oils and must be stored in the refrigerator if kept longer than 1 month.
3. Peanut oil may also be frozen.
4. According to the Texas Peanut Producers Board, peanut oil may be used 3 or 4 times to fry turkeys before signs of deterioration begin.
5. Such indications include foaming, darkening, or smoking excessively, indicating oil must be discarded.
6. Other signs of deteriorated oil include a rancid smell and/or failure to bubble when food is added.

Brine Method of Cooking Turkey

Brining is a pretreatment in which the whole turkey is placed in a salt and water solution known as brine. This pretreatment produces a wonderfully moist and well-seasoned bird. Brining should be done in the refrigerator or in a cooler with 5 to 6 ice packs to keep turkey and brine at 40 degrees F. or below during the entire brining process. Brining is more manageable with a rather small turkey, from 12 to 14 pounds, but you can brine a 24-pound turkey if you have the room.

Table salt or kosher salt can be used to make brine. Crystal kosher salt is recommended since table salt contains additives such as anti-caking ingredients, iodine, and other additives. Table salt is also very finely ground and more is required to produce good results, so be sure and use crystal kosher salt.

Directions:

1. Start brining method the day before you plan to cook the turkey.
2. Wash fresh or completely thawed turkey inside and out, and remove giblet bag and neck.
3. In large stockpot, plastic tub, or cooler, dissolve 2 cups crystal kosher salt in 2 gallons cold water
4. Add 1 cup sugar.
5. Stir until salt and sugar are completely dissolved.
6. Herbs and spices may be added to brine to enhance flavor.
7. Add several crushed bay leaves, several sprigs of dried thyme, or other dried herbs, if desired.
8. Place turkey in brine solution, breast down.
9. Cover and chill for 6 to 8 hours.
10. To use overnight method, reduce salt and sugar amounts by ½ so turkey does not retain too much salt.
11. Remove turkey from brine, rinse inside and out under cold running water, and pat dry with paper towels.
12. Place on shallow pan and refrigerate overnight. (This allows skin to dry out so it becomes crisp during roasting. This step may be omitted if desired.)

13. Preheat oven to 350 degrees F.
14. Place turkey in shallow roasting pan.
15. Tie legs together and tuck wings underneath bird.
16. Coat skin with butter or olive oil.
17. Cover breast loosely with aluminum foil.
18. Add 1 cup water to bottom of pan.
19. Check wrapper for weight of turkey; see chart on page 202 to determine approximate cooking time.
20. Roast turkey until temperature in thickest part of thigh reaches 165 degrees F. or thigh juices run clear when pierced with a fork.
21. During the last 1 to 1½ hours of cooking time, remove aluminum foil from breast, and baste with pan juices to encourage browning.
22. Add more water to pan if necessary.
23. When turkey is done, allow to sit 20 minutes before carving to allow juices to saturate meat evenly.

Braised Turkey

Braising is cooking the turkey in a small amount of water or stock in a covered roasting pan. Braising is a moist-heat method similar to the oven-cooking bag method. This method creates a moist, tender turkey.

Directions:

1. Preheat oven to 325 to 350 degrees F.
2. Cavity of turkey can be filled with onions, celery, and other vegetables for added flavor.
3. Use roasting pan large enough to accommodate turkey; lid must fit snugly on pan.
4. Insert meat thermometer in thickest part of thigh, and cook to 165 degrees F.
5. Pour off cooking liquid that accumulates in bottom of pan and use for side dish of dressing.
6. Turkey will brown lightly during braising.

Smoked Turkey

Most smokers are cylinder-shaped devices and use electricity, gas, or charcoal for heat. Follow the manufacturer's directions for gas or electric smokers. The USDA Food Safety and Inspection Service recommends the following pointers for smoking a turkey.

1. Turkey breasts, drumsticks, wings, and whole turkeys are all suited for smoking.
2. Whole turkeys that weigh 12 pounds or less are the recommended size for safe smoking. (A larger turkey remains in the "Danger Zone" – between 40 degrees F. and 140 degrees F. – for too long.)
3. If a larger turkey has been mistakenly purchased, detach dark meat sections (leg and thigh portions) from breast, and smoke turkey parts separately for best results.
4. There should be at least 1 inch of space between turkey and lid of smoker.
5. Do not stuff turkey, because smoking is at a low temperature and it can take too long for temperature of stuffing to reach required temperature of 165 degrees F. (Also, smoked stuffing has an undesirable flavor.)

Charcoal Smoker:

1. Fill pan for liquid with water, wine, apple juice, or the liquid you desire.
2. Fill charcoal pan with good quality charcoal.
3. Light charcoal and place cover on smoker.
4. When smoker has reached an internal temperature of 250 to 300 degrees F., quickly place turkey on smoker rack and replace cover.
5. Add charcoal every hour, as necessary, to maintain 250 to 300 degrees F.; replenish liquid as necessary.
6. Heat and liquid are critical to maintaining the hot smoke that cooks the turkey.
7. To enhance flavors, add chunks or chips of water-soaked hardwood or fruitwood.

8. DO NOT use softwood (pine, fir, cedar, or spruce) as it gives food a turpentine flavor and coats it with a black pitch or resin.
9. Smoking time depends on many factors: size and shape of turkey, distance from heat, temperature of coals, and outside air temperature.
10. Estimate 20 to 30 minutes per pound when smoking.
11. Always use a food thermometer.
12. Whole turkey is done when food thermometer placed in inner thigh reaches 165 degrees F.
13. Breast is done when internal temperature reaches 170 degrees F.

Oven Cooking Bag Roasted Turkey

Preparing a turkey in an oven cooking bag can be a safe and delicious alternative to the traditional roasting method. This method produces a moist-heat cooking environment. In this technique a large, heat-tempered plastic cooking bag especially designed for oven temperatures is used. Bags can be purchased in the paper goods section of most grocery stores. Instructions for use are printed on the box.

Directions:

1. Preheat oven to 350 degrees F.
2. To prevent bursting add 1 tablespoon of dry flour to bag and shake to coat.
3. Cut slits in bag to allow steam to escape.
4. Use a roasting pan large enough so bag does not hang over sides.
5. Allow ample space for bag to expand during cooking so it does not touch top or sides of oven or it will melt.
6. Insert meat thermometer through plastic into thickest part of thigh.
7. Turkey is done when temperature reaches 165 degrees F.

Citrus-Marinated Grilled Turkey

This is a delicious marinade for turkey.

Ingredients for citrus marinade:

4   tangerines, clementines, or oranges
1   head garlic, halved
4   sprigs fresh rosemary
4   sprigs fresh thyme
1   Tbs. whole black peppercorns
    extra-virgin olive oil

Ingredients for turkey:

1   turkey (12 to 14 lb.)
    extra-virgin olive oil
    salt and freshly ground black pepper
    citrus marinade (recipe below)

Directions for citrus marinade:

1. Put all marinade ingredients in bowl and pour in a generous amount of olive oil.
2. Squeeze together with your hands to blend all flavors.

Directions for turkey:

1. Cut turkey into 4 pieces and remove bones from breast (save neck and backbone for gravy).
2. To marinate, put turkey on large platter and pour on marinade.
3. Turn turkey over in marinade to make sure it is well coated on both sides.
4. Cover with plastic wrap and refrigerate for at least 2 hours or overnight.
5. Remove turkey from refrigerator about ½ hour before ready to grill.
6. Heat grill to medium and wipe grate with oil.
7. Wipe marinade from turkey.

8. Season turkey with salt and pepper.
9. Put turkey on grill, skin side down, and cook for 30 minutes.
10. Turn bird over and continue grilling, basting with more olive oil, until juices run clear and internal temperature of thigh is 165 degrees F., about 1 hour total.
11. Set aside, cover with foil, and let rest about 10 minutes before carving.

Herbed Turkey Breast

The herb butter basting sauce keeps this turkey breast moist, and it is easy to carve.

Ingredients:

½   c. butter
¼   c. lemon juice
2   Tbs. soy sauce
2   Tbs. finely chopped green onion
1   Tbs. rubbed sage
1   tsp. dried thyme
1   tsp. dried marjoram
¼   tsp. pepper
1   bone-in, whole turkey breast (5½ to 6 lb.)

Directions:

1. Preheat oven to 325 degrees F.
2. In small saucepan combine first 8 ingredients; bring to a boil then remove from heat.
3. Place turkey in shallow roasting pan; baste with butter mixture.
4. Bake uncovered for 1½ to 2 hours or until meat thermometer reads 170 degrees F., basting every 30 minutes.

Yields: 10 to 12 servings.

Grilled Turkey Mole

This is a wonderful way to serve turkey. The chocolate in this recipe adds a whole new flavor to the meat.

Ingredients:

6   turkey breast tenderloins, rinsed, dried
¼   c. lime juice
1   Tbs. chili powder
2   tsp. hot pepper sauce
1   Tbs. butter
½   c. chopped onion
2   tsp. sugar
1   clove garlic, minced
7   oz. canned tomatoes, undrained, cut up
¼   c. canned diced green chili peppers
1½ tsp. unsweetened cocoa powder
1½ tsp. chili powder
⅛   tsp. salt
    sour cream

Directions:

1. In small bowl stir together lime juice, 1 tablespoon chili powder, and hot pepper sauce.
2. Pour over turkey in resealable plastic food storage bag.
3. Marinate in refrigerator for 2 to 4 hours, turning bag occasionally.
4. In medium saucepan over high heat, cook and stir onion, sugar, and garlic in butter about 7 minutes or until onion is tender.
5. Stir in undrained tomatoes, chili peppers, cocoa powder, chili powder, and salt.
6. Bring to boiling; reduce heat.
7. Cover and simmer for 10 minutes.
8. Remove from heat; set aside.
9. Drain turkey, discarding marinade.

10. Grill turkey on lightly greased rack of uncovered grill directly over medium coals for 8 to 10 minutes or until turkey is tender and no longer pink, turning once.
11. Serve with mole sauce and sour cream.

Yields: 6 servings.

Aluminum Foil Wrapped Roasted Turkey

Wrapping and cooking entire turkey in aluminum foil requires increased oven temperature to ensure safety. This method actually steams the turkey in its own juices. It produces a moist bird with a light golden, non-crisp skin. The cooking time is reduced due to higher temperatures and the trapped steam inside the foil.

Directions:

1. Preheat oven to 450 degrees F.
2. Brush turkey with melted butter.
3. Tear off a piece of 18-inch-wide heavy-duty aluminum foil that is 3 times longer than the turkey.
4. Place turkey lengthwise in middle of foil, breast side up; bring foil ends up, overlapping turkey.
5. Insert meat thermometer through foil into thickest part of thigh.
6. Place turkey in shallow roasting pan and bring sides of foil up around turkey. (Do not make an airtight seal.)
7. To brown turkey, open foil during last 30 minutes of cooking.
8. Reserve broth for moistening stuffing or for making giblet gravy.
9. Cooking time can be reduced by as much as 30 minutes to an hour compared to traditional roasting timetable.

Smoked Turkey on the Grill

Here is a way to prepare a great smoked turkey if you do not have a smoker.

Ingredients:

1	turkey (12 lb. or less)
2	qt. apple juice
1	lb. brown sugar
1	c. kosher salt
3	qt. water
3	oranges, quartered
4	oz. fresh ginger, thinly sliced
15	whole cloves
6	bay leaves
6	lg. cloves garlic, crushed
	cooking string for trussing turkey
	roasting rack
	heavy-gauge foil pan
	hickory chips

Directions:

1. Combine apple juice, brown sugar, and salt in large saucepan; bring to a boil and continue heating until sugar and salt have dissolved.
2. Skim off any foam that forms on top; cool.
3. In large (5 gallons or more) stock pot or similar container, combine apple juice mixture, 3 quarts water, oranges, ginger, cloves, bay leaves, and garlic.
4. Wash turkey; remove any fatty deposits and everything from body cavity.
5. Place turkey in brine mixture; refrigerate for 24 hours.
6. Make sure turkey remains completely submerged.
7. At least 1 hour before grilling, soak woodchips in enough water to cover.
8. Arrange medium-hot coals around drip pan.
9. Drain wood chips.
10. Remove turkey from brine; pat dry with paper towels.
11. Tie legs together with string, and lightly brush turkey with vegetable oil.
12. Place turkey on roasting rack inside foil pan.

13. Place on grill away from direct heat.
14. Sprinkle half of wood chips over coals.
15. After 30 to 40 minutes, wrap wings in foil to keep them from burning.
16. Sprinkle coals with remaining chips.
17. Brush with vegetable oil periodically.
18. If breast starts to get too brown, cover with foil.
19. Turkey is done when internal temperature reaches 165 degrees F. in the thigh or 170 degrees F. in the breast (will take about 12 to 14 minutes per pound).
20. When done, remove from grill and let rest about 15 minutes before carving.

Spiced Mustard-Glazed Ham

In case you do not want to serve turkey or you want to have a second meat dish, try this easy glazed ham recipe. It makes an attractive and decorative ham.

Ingredients:

1   fully cooked ham, boneless (about 5 lb.)
1   jar orange marmalade (16 to 18 oz. or make your own using recipe on page 186)
1   Tbs. plus 2 tsp. dry mustard
½   c. spicy brown mustard
1   clove garlic, minced
½   tsp. ground ginger

Directions:

1. Preheat oven to 350 degrees F.
2. Place ham on rack in roasting pan, fat side up.
3. Score fat of ham in diamond pattern.
4. Combine remaining ingredients, stirring until well blended; refrigerate half of mixture.
5. Brush ham with remaining half of mixture.
6. Bake for about 2 hours or until meat thermometer registers 140 degrees F.
7. Brush with reserved marmalade mixture every 15 to 20 minutes.

Yields: About 10 servings.

Spiced Apple Cider Brined Turkey

This brine adds flavor and moistness to your turkey.

Ingredients for brine:

- 4 c. water
- ½ c. kosher salt
- ½ c. sugar
- 3 whole cloves
- 1 tsp. black peppercorns, cracked
- 2 bay leaves, broken into pieces
- 4 slices fresh gingerroot
- 1 tsp. whole allspice, crushed
- ½ gal. unsweetened apple cider, chilled (8 c.)
- 1 turkey (12 to 14 lb.), fresh or completely thawed
- 2 turkey-size oven cooking bags or large plastic tub

Directions for brine:

1. Use mortar and pestle or spice grinder to crush whole peppercorns and allspice. Do not grind to a powder; large pieces should remain.
2. In 4-quart saucepan combine water, salt, sugar, cloves, peppercorns, bay leaves, and ginger.
3. Stir as you bring mixture to a boil over medium-high heat; boil gently for 2 minutes then remove from heat.
4. Add chilled apple cider; stir to combine.
5. Refrigerate brine while preparing turkey.
6. Remove turkey from wrapper.
7. Remove giblets and neck from body cavity and neck area; refrigerate for stock for making gravy.
8. Rinse turkey inside and out under cold running water.
9. Twist wing tips and tuck behind turkey.
10. Place one plastic oven-cooking bag inside the other.
11. Set bags in large stockpot or roasting pan (or use large plastic tub, bags not needed.)
12. Roll top of bags over for ease in handling; place turkey, breast first, inside double thickness of bags.
13. Do not use trash bags or any bag that is not food safe (chemicals from bag will leach into turkey).

14. Pour chilled brine into turkey cavity and around outside of turkey.
15. Pour an additional 2 cups cold water around turkey.
16. Secure bag with twist tie.
17. If using roasting pan, turn turkey breast down.
18. Rotate turkey 4 times during brining so brine reaches all parts.
19. If using stockpot, brine should cover turkey and rotation is not needed.
20. Refrigerate turkey 12 to 14 hours.
21. Remove turkey from brine; rinse under cold running water; rinse well inside and out.
22. Pat skin dry with towels.
23. Place turkey on platter and refrigerate for several hours or overnight. (This will allow skin to dry. Skin will be very crisp with this drying step, however, this step can be omitted. Turkey skin will still brown, but will be less crispy.)

Directions for baking:

1. Preheat oven to 350 degrees F.
2. Transfer turkey to heavy roasting pan.
3. Position meat thermometer in thickest part of thigh.
4. Tie legs together and tuck wings underneath bird.
5. Cover skin with softened butter or olive oil.
6. Add 1 cup water to bottom of pan and place turkey in hot oven.
7. Check wrapper and cook according to weight.
8. Roast turkey until temperature in thickest part of thigh reaches 165 degrees F. or thigh juices run clear when pricked with long-tined fork or leg wiggles freely in joint.
9. After 2 hours of roasting, baste turkey with some of pan drippings, if desired.
10. If skin is browning too quickly, cover with aluminum foil during last hour of cooking time.
11. Resist the urge to open oven during roasting time since loss of heat and moisture will interfere with roasting time.
12. When turkey is done (165 degrees F.), allow bird to sit 20 to 30 minutes before carving to allow juices to redistribute evenly through meat.
13. Reserve pan juices for use in gravy, dressing, etc.
14. Store leftover turkey promptly after the meal.

Chipotle-Rubbed Smoked Turkey

Chipotle is a popular flavor with many people, and this is a nice variation for the chipotle lovers.

Ingredients:

1 turkey breast half with bone (2 to 2½ lb.)
3 c. hickory or mesquite wood chips
1 tsp. ground coriander
½ tsp. paprika
¼ tsp. black pepper
1 sm. dried chipotle pepper, seeded, crushed (or ⅛ to ¼ tsp. cayenne pepper)
2 tsp. olive oil
fresh cilantro
fresh chili peppers

Directions:

1. Thaw turkey if frozen.
2. At least 1 hour before grilling, soak woodchips in enough water to cover.
3. Meanwhile, in small bowl combine coriander, paprika, black pepper, and chipotle pepper.
4. Remove skin and excess fat from turkey breast.
5. Brush turkey with oil; rub with spice mixture.
6. Insert meat thermometer into thickest part of turkey. (Do not allow thermometer tip to touch bone.)
7. Drain wood chips.
8. For charcoal grill: arrange medium-hot coals around drip pan.
9. Sprinkle half of wood chips over coals.
10. Test for medium heat above pan.
11. Place turkey, bone side down, in roasting pan on grill rack over drip pan.
12. Cover and grill for 45 minutes.
13. Sprinkle coals with remaining chips.
14. Cover and grill for 45 minutes to 1¼ hours more or until thermometer registers 170 degrees F.
15. Add more coals as needed.

16. Remove turkey from grill, and cover loosely with foil; let stand 10 minutes before slicing.
17. If desired, garnish with cilantro and fresh chili peppers.
18. For gas grill: Preheat grill.
19. Reduce heat to medium; adjust for indirect cooking.
20. Add drained wood chips according to manufacturer's directions.
21. Place turkey in roasting pan on grill rack over unlit burner; grill as above.

Yields: 8 to 10 servings.

Smoked or Baked Spare Ribs

It is more likely that the early settlers ate spare ribs for Thanksgiving instead of our traditional turkey. These delicious ribs can be cooked on the grill or in the oven.

Ingredients for ribs:

6 lb. pork spareribs
½ c. brown sugar, firmly packed
2 Tbs. chili powder
1 Tbs. paprika
1 Tbs. freshly ground black pepper
2 Tbs. garlic powder
2 tsp. onion powder
2 tsp. kosher salt
2 tsp. ground cumin
1 tsp. ground cinnamon
2 c. wood chips, soaked

Ingredients for sauce:

1 c. apple cider
¾ c. cider vinegar
1 Tbs. onion powder

1   Tbs. garlic powder
2   Tbs. lemon juice
1   jalapeno pepper, finely chopped (optional)
3   Tbs. hot pepper sauce
     kosher salt and freshly ground black pepper to taste

Directions for ribs:

1. In medium bowl mix together brown sugar, chili powder, paprika, pepper, garlic powder, onion powder, salt, cumin, and cinnamon.
2. Rub generously onto pork spareribs.
3. Cover, and refrigerate for at least 4 hours or overnight.
4. Prepare outdoor grill for indirect heat, or preheat smoker to 250 degrees F.
5. When coals are gray and ashed over, place 2 handfuls of soaked woodchips directly on them.
6. Place ribs on grill grate, bone side down.
7. Cover, and cook for 3½ to 4 hours, adding more coals as needed.
8. Baste with sauce, and throw handfuls of soaked woodchips onto coals every hour.
9. Keep temperature of grill or smoker from going below 225 degrees F.
10. Ribs are done when the rub has created a wonderful crispy blackened "bark" and meat has pulled away from bone.
11. Discard any leftover sauce.
12. Or, if you prefer, bake in oven, covered, at 350 degrees F. for 3 hours.

Directions for sauce:

1. While grill heats up, prepare sauce.
2. In medium bowl stir together all ingredients.

Yields: 6 servings.

Thanksgiving Delights Cookbook

A Collection of Thanksgiving Recipes
Cookbook Delights Holiday Series Book 11

Pies

Table of Contents

Did You Know? . . . .

Did you know that in Mexico, turkey meat with mole sauce is widely regarded as the unofficial national dish?

A Basic Recipe for Pie Crust

This is a very good recipe for a delicious, flaky crust.

Ingredients for single crust:

> 1½ c. sifted all-purpose flour
> ½   tsp. salt
> ½   c. shortening
> 4-5 Tbs. ice water

Ingredients for double crust:

> 2   c. sifted all-purpose flour
> 1   tsp. salt
> ⅔   c. shortening
> 5-7 Tbs. ice water

Directions for single crust:

1. In large bowl stir together flour and salt.
2. Cut in shortening with pastry blender or mix with fingertips until pieces are size of coarse crumbs.
3. Sprinkle 2 tablespoons ice water over flour mixture, tossing with fork.
4. Add just enough remaining water 1 tablespoon at a time to moisten dough, tossing so dough holds together.
5. Roll pastry into 11-inch circle and wrap in plastic wrap; refrigerate for 1 hour.
6. Preheat oven to 425 degrees F.
7. Remove plastic wrap from pastry, and fit pastry into a 9-inch pie plate.
8. Fold edge under and then crimp between thumb and forefinger to make fluted crust.
9. For filled pie with an instant or cooked filling (cream-filled, custard-filled, etc.), prick crust all over with fork then bake 15 to 20 minutes until done.
10. If preparing pie with uncooked filling (such as pumpkin), do not prick crust; pour filling into unbaked pastry shell, and then bake as directed.

Directions for double crust:

1. Turn desired filling into pastry-lined pie plate; trim overhanging edge of pastry ½ inch from rim of plate.
2. Cut slits with knife in top crust for steam vents.
3. Place over filling; trim overhanging edge of pastry 1 inch from rim of plate.
4. Fold and roll top edge under lower edge, pressing on rim to seal; flute.
5. Cover fluted edge with 2- to 3-inch-wide strip of aluminum foil to prevent excessive browning.
6. Remove foil during last 15 minutes of baking.

Yields: 1 pie crust (9-inch single or double).

A Basic Cookie or Graham Cracker Crust

This is a great crust for use with cream pies or for an unbaked pie. Use your favorite flavor of cookie to complement your filling, or use graham crackers.

Ingredients:

2 c. cookie or graham cracker crumbs, finely crushed
⅓ c. sugar
½ c. butter, melted

Directions:

1. Combine crumbs, sugar, and butter.
2. Press mixture firmly against bottom and up sides of 9-inch pie plate.
3. Baking is not necessary, but if preferred crust may be baked at 400 degrees F. for 10 minutes.

Yields: 1 pie crust (9-inch).

Cranberry Apple Pie

This is a delicious twist to the traditional apple pie. It is wonderful when served warm with vanilla ice cream.

Ingredients for filling:

1	unbaked 9-inch pastry shell (recipe page 224)
1¼	c. sugar
¼	c. all-purpose flour
¼	tsp. salt
2	c. cranberries
¼	c. maple syrup
5	tart apples, peeled, cored, sliced
½	c. chopped walnuts

Ingredients for topping:

1	c. dry bread crumbs
¾	c. all-purpose flour
¼	c. brown sugar, firmly packed
¼	c. butter, melted

Directions for filling:

1. Prepare pastry shell.
2. Preheat oven to 375 degrees F.
3. In large saucepan mix together sugar, flour, and salt.
4. Stir in cranberries and maple syrup; cook over high heat, stirring constantly.
5. When mixture comes to a boil, reduce heat, cover, and simmer 5 minutes, stirring occasionally.
6. Stir apples into simmering mixture, and continue to cook for 5 minutes or until apples are tender.
7. Remove from heat; stir in walnuts.
8. Pour apple mixture into prepared pie shell; set aside.

Directions for topping:

1. In medium bowl combine bread crumbs, flour, brown sugar, and melted butter.
2. Mix well; sprinkle over apple filling.
3. Bake 30 minutes or until topping is golden brown.

Yields: 6 to 8 servings.

Cranberry Cream Pie

The tang of cranberries meets the rich goodness of whipped cream in this cream pie. It is very attractive and is great in that it can be made ahead.

Ingredients:

- 1   baked 9-inch single-crust pastry shell (recipe page 224)
- 2   c. boiling water
- 1   c. dried cranberries
- 1   c. sugar
- ½   c. all-purpose flour
- 2¼ c. milk
- 2   eggs, lightly beaten
- ½   c. sour cream
- ¼   c. butter, diced
- 1   c. heavy whipping cream
- 3   Tbs. confectioners' sugar
- 1   tsp. vanilla extract

Directions:

1. Prepare baked pastry shell according to recipe directions; set aside.
2. Pour boiling water over cranberries to cover.
3. Let stand 5 minutes then drain.
4. In medium heavy-bottom saucepan, combine sugar and flour.
5. Gradually stir in milk and eggs.
6. Cook over medium heat, stirring constantly, until mixture thickens and boils.
7. Boil and stir for 2 minutes; remove from heat.
8. Stir in sour cream, butter, and cranberries; pour mixture into baked pastry shell.
9. Cover with plastic wrap, and refrigerate for several hours or overnight.
10. Whip cream until soft peaks form.
11. Fold in confectioners' sugar and vanilla.
12. Swirl over top of cooled pie.

Yields: 6 to 8 servings.

Custard Pie

This was one of my dad's favorite pies.

Ingredients:

1	unbaked 9-inch pastry shell (recipe page 224)
4	eggs
½	c. sugar
¼	tsp. salt
1	tsp. vanilla extract
2½	c. milk
¼	tsp. ground nutmeg

Directions for crust:

1. Preheat oven to 450 degrees F.
2. Prepare pastry shell.
3. Line with double thickness of heavy-duty foil.
4. Bake for 8 minutes.
5. Remove foil; bake 5 minutes longer.
6. Remove from oven and set aside.

Directions for custard:

1. After baking crust, reduce oven temperature to 350 degrees F.
2. Separate 1 egg; set white aside.
3. In mixing bowl beat yolk and remaining eggs just until combined.
4. Blend in sugar, salt, and vanilla; stir in milk.
5. Beat reserved egg white until stiff peaks form; fold into egg mixture.
6. Carefully pour into crust.
7. Cover edges of pie with foil and bake 25 minutes.
8. Remove foil; bake 15 to 20 minutes longer or until knife inserted near center comes out clean.
9. Cool on wire rack.
10. Sprinkle with nutmeg.
11. Store in refrigerator.

Yields: 6 to 8 servings.

Huckleberry Custard Pie

This is an excellent dessert pie and a family favorite.

Ingredients for pastry:

  2¼ c. all-purpose flour
  1   tsp. salt
  ⅔   c. vegetable oil
  4   Tbs. cold water

Ingredients for filling:

  4   eggs, slightly beaten
  ½   c. half-and-half
  1¾ c. sugar
  ¼   c. all-purpose flour
  4   c. huckleberries

Directions for pastry:

  1. Combine flour and salt in bowl.
  2. Blend in oil with fork.
  3. Sprinkle water over mixture; toss.
  4. Shape dough into 2 balls; flatten slightly.
  5. Roll one portion into circle between 2 pieces wax paper; peel paper off top.
  6. Place pastry in 8- or 9-inch pie plate.
  7. Reserve remaining dough for lattice top.

Directions for filling:

  1. Preheat oven to 375 degrees F.
  2. Mix together eggs and half-and-half.
  3. Stir in sugar and flour.
  4. Mix in huckleberries.
  5. Pour into pastry-lined pie plate.
  6. Cover with lattice top.
  7. Bake for 50 to 60 minutes or until nicely browned.

Yields: 8 servings.

Mince Pie

This dessert, long favored by the British at holiday time, originally contained minced meat along with the fruits and spices. This version is meatless and brimming with apples, dried fruit, and lots of spices.

Ingredients:

3½ lb. small pippin apples, peeled, cored, chopped
½   c. chopped pitted prunes
½   c. golden raisins
½   c. dried currants
½   c. dark brown sugar, firmly packed
¼   c. unsulphured (light) molasses
¼   c. brandy
¼   c. orange juice
¼   c. unsalted butter, cut into pieces
2   Tbs. dark rum
1   Tbs. grated orange peel
1   tsp. grated lemon peel
1   tsp. ground cinnamon
¼   tsp. ground cloves
¼   tsp. ground allspice
¼   tsp. ground nutmeg
1   pinch of salt
1   double-crust pastry recipe (recipe page 224)

Directions:

1. Combine all ingredients except pastry in large, heavy saucepan or Dutch oven.
2. Cook over low heat until apples are very tender and mixture is thick, stirring occasionally, about 1½ hours.
3. Cool filling completely. (Can be prepared up to 1 week ahead. Cover and refrigerate.)

4. Preheat oven to 400 degrees F.
5. Prepare pastry; line 9-inch pie plate with half of pastry.
6. Spoon filling into crust-lined pan, gently pressing flat.
7. Top pie with remaining pastry or make lattice top; flute edge and brush crust with milk.
8. Bake until crust is golden brown and mince bubbles, about 40 minutes.
9. Cool completely.

Yields: 8 servings.

Frozen Pumpkin Pie

This is a cool, refreshing alternative to the traditional pumpkin pie.

Ingredients:

1   graham cracker crust (recipe page 225)
3   c. vanilla ice cream, softened
1   c. cooked or canned pumpkin
½   c. brown sugar, firmly packed
¼   tsp. salt
¼   tsp. ground cinnamon
¼   tsp. ground ginger
¼   tsp. ground nutmeg

Directions:

1. Prepare 9-inch graham cracker crust; cool.
2. In mixing bowl combine ice cream, pumpkin, brown sugar, salt, and spices; mix well.
3. Pour into cooled crust.
4. Freeze for 4 hours or until firm.

Yields: 6 to 8 servings.

Pecan Apple Pie

This is a delicious pie with caramel sauce to enjoy for the holidays.

Ingredients for filling:

- 1   c. sugar
- ⅓   c. all-purpose flour
- 2   tsp. ground cinnamon
- ¼   tsp. salt
- 12 c. peeled, thinly sliced tart apples (about 10 apples)
- 1   double-crust pastry recipe (see recipe page 224)

Ingredients for topping:

- 1   c. brown sugar, firmly packed
- ½   c. all-purpose flour
- ¾   c. rolled oats
- ½   c. cold butter
- 1   c. chopped pecans
- ½   c. caramel sauce (recipe below)

Ingredients for caramel sauce:

- 1   c. sugar
- ½   c. water
- 1   c. heavy cream
- 1   tsp. vanilla extract

Directions for filling:

1. Line two 9-inch pie plates with pastry.
2. Trim and flute edges; set aside.
3. Preheat oven to 375 degrees F.
4. In large bowl combine sugar, flour, cinnamon, and salt; add apples and toss to coat.
5. Pour into pastry shells.

Directions for topping:

1. Combine brown sugar, flour, and oats; cut in butter until crumbly.
2. Sprinkle over apples.
3. Cover edges loosely with foil.
4. Bake for 25 minutes.
5. Remove foil; bake 25 to 30 minutes longer or until filling is bubbly.
6. Sprinkle with pecans.
7. Drizzle with caramel sauce.
8. Cool on wire racks.

Directions for caramel sauce:

1. Place cream in small saucepan over low heat.
2. Cover and keep warm while making caramel.
3. Combine sugar and water in large, heavy saucepan; bring to a boil.
4. Brush down any sugar crystals that form on side of pan with wet pastry brush.
5. Once mixture caramelizes to a golden brown, remove from heat.
6. Slowly add warm cream to caramel.
7. Return pan to low heat and stir until caramel dissolves into cream completely.
8. Let simmer for 2 minutes.
9. Remove from heat and stir in vanilla.
10. Drizzle while still hot.

Yields: 2 pies (6 to 8 servings each).

Did You Know? . . . .

Did you know that fresh cranberries can be frozen at home and will keep up to nine months? They can be used directly in recipes without thawing.

Thanksgiving Butterscotch Pie

Some of my children love butterscotch, and they really enjoy this pie.

Ingredients for filling:

1   baked 9-inch single-crust pastry shell (see recipe page 224)
1   c. light brown sugar, firmly packed
¼   c. cornstarch
½   tsp. salt
⅔   c. water
2   c. milk
⅓   c. butter
4   egg yolks (reserve 3 whites for meringue)
1½ tsp. vanilla extract

Ingredients for meringue:

3   egg whites
¼   tsp. cream of tartar
6   Tbs. sugar

Directions for filling:

1. Prepare baked pastry shell.
2. Mix brown sugar, cornstarch, and salt in saucepan.
3. Gradually stir in water and milk; add butter.
4. Cook over medium heat, stirring constantly, until mixture thickens and boils; boil for 1 minute.
5. Remove from heat.
6. Slightly beat egg yolks.
7. Gradually stir at least ½ of mixture into beaten egg yolks.
8. Blend into remaining mixture in pan.
9. Boil mixture for 1 minute, stirring constantly.
10. Remove pan from heat; blend in vanilla.
11. Pour mixture into baked pie crust.

Directions for meringue:

1. Preheat oven to 400 degrees F.
2. In medium bowl add cream of tartar to egg whites.

3. Beat until frothy.
4. Gradually beat in sugar a little at a time, beating until stiff and glossy.
5. Spread meringue over hot pie filling.
6. To prevent weeping or shrinking, tightly seal meringue to edge of crust.
7. Bake for 8 to 10 minutes, until meringue is golden.

Yields: 6 to 8 servings.

Blackberry Sour Cream Pie

One of my favorite berries is the blackberry, and blackberries and sour cream make a great combination.

Ingredients:

1   qt. blackberries, fresh or frozen, unthawed
½   c. plus 2 Tbs. sugar, divided
¼   c. all-purpose flour
1   c. sour cream
1   deep-dish 9-inch pastry shell, unbaked (recipe page 224)

Directions:

1. Preheat oven to 350 degrees F.
2. Wash fresh berries and spread out to dry.
3. Thoroughly mix together ½ cup sugar and flour.
4. Pour over berries and toss to cover completely, ensuring flour mixture is evenly distributed.
5. Pour berries into pie shell and spread, mounding berries slightly in center.
6. Mix sour cream with 2 tablespoons sugar, and drop by tablespoonfuls over pie.
7. Tent pie lightly with aluminum foil, and bake for about 1 hour.
8. Remove foil, and continue to bake about 15 minutes or until lightly browned.
9. Serve either warm or cold.

Yields: 8 servings.

Pumpkin Pie

This is a family favorite and is delicious served cold with sweetened whipped cream or warm with vanilla bean ice cream.

Ingredients:

2	unbaked 9-inch single-crust pastry shells (recipe page 224)
8	eggs
1	can solid-pack pumpkin (29 oz.)
2	c. brown sugar, firmly packed
2	tsp. ground cinnamon
1	tsp. salt
½	tsp. ground cloves
½	tsp. ground nutmeg
½	tsp. ground ginger
2½	c. evaporated milk

Directions for filling:

1. Preheat oven to 450 degrees F.
2. Prepare pastry shells; set aside.
3. Beat eggs in mixing bowl.
4. Add pumpkin, sugar, cinnamon, salt, cloves, nutmeg, and ginger; beat just until smooth.
5. Gradually stir in milk.
6. Pour into pastry shells and bake for 10 minutes.
7. Reduce heat to 350 degrees F., and bake 40 to 45 minutes longer or until knife inserted near center comes out clean.
8. Cool on wire racks.
9. If desired, cut pastry scraps with 1-inch leaf-shaped cookie cutter; place on ungreased baking sheet.
10. Bake at 350 degrees F. for 10 to 15 minutes or until lightly browned; place on baked pies as garnish.

Yields: 2 pies (6 to 8 servings each).

Thanksgiving Delights Cookbook

A Collection of Thanksgiving Recipes
Cookbook Delights Holiday Series Book 11

Preserving

Table of Contents

Did You Know? . . . .

Did you know that the young leaves and vine tips of sweet potatoes are widely consumed as a vegetable in some West African countries?

A Basic Guide for Canning,

Dehydrating, and Freezing

1. Place empty jars in hot, soapy water. Wash well inside and out with brush or soft cloth.
2. Run your finger around rim of each jar, discarding any that are chipped or cracked.
3. Rinse in clean, clear, very hot water, being careful to use tongs to avoid burning skin or fingers.
4. Place upside down on towel or fabric to drain well.
5. Place lids in boiling water bath for 2 minutes to sterilize and keep hot until ready to place on jar rims.
6. Immediately prior to filling jars with hot food, immerse in hot bath for 1 minute to heat jars. Heating jars avoids breakage.
7. If filling with room-temperature food, you need not immerse immediately prior to filling.
8. Fill jars with food to within ½ inch of neck of jars.
9. When ladling liquid over food, fill jars to 1 inch from top rim in each jar. This leaves air allowance for sealing purposes.
10. Wipe rims of jars with damp, clean cloth to remove any particles of food and again check for chips or cracks.
11. Using tongs, place lids from hot bath directly onto jars.
12. Place rings over lids, and using cloth, gloves, or holders, tighten down firmly while hanging onto jars.
13. Do not tighten down too hard as air may become trapped in jars and prevent them from sealing.
14. For fruits, tomatoes, and pickled vegetables, place each jar into water bath canning kettle so water covers jars by at least 1 inch.
15. For vegetables, process them in a pressure canner according to manufacturer's directions.
16. Follow time recommended for food being canned.
17. Do not mix jars of food in same canning kettle as times may vary for each kind of food.
18. At end of time recommended for canning, gently lift

each jar out of bath with tongs, and place on protected surface.
19. Turn lids gently to be sure they are firmly tight.
20. Place filled, ringed jars on cloth to cool gradually.
21. Do not disturb rings, lids, or jars until sealed.
22. Lids will show slight indentation when sealed.
23. When cool, wipe jars with damp cloth then label and date each jar.
24. Leave overnight until thoroughly cooled.
25. Jars may then be stored upright on shelves.

Dehydrating

1. Always begin with fresh, good quality food that is clean and inspected for damage.
2. Pretreatment is not necessary, but food that is blanched will keep its color and flavor better. Use the same blanching times as you would for freezing. Fruit, especially, responds well to pretreatment.
3. Doing some research on pretreatments may help you decide what procedure you would like to use.
4. You can marinate, salt, sweeten, or spice foods before you dehydrate them.
5. Jerky is meat that has been marinated and/or flavored by rubbing spices into it; avoid oil or grease of any kind as it will turn rancid as the food dries.
6. Vegetables and fruit can be treated the same way.
7. Slice or dice food thin and uniform so that it will dehydrate evenly. Uneven thicknesses may cause food to spoil because it did not dry as thoroughly as other parts.
8. Space food on dehydrator tray so that air can move around each piece.
9. Try not to let any piece touch another.
10. Fill your trays with all the same type of food as different foods take different amounts of time to dry.
11. You can, of course, dry different types of food at the

same time, but you will have to remember to watch and remove the food that dehydrates more quickly. You can mix different foods in the same dehydrator batch, but do not mix strong vegetables like onions and garlic as other foods will absorb their taste while they are dehydrating.

12. The smaller the pieces, the faster a food will dehydrate. Thin leaves of spinach, celery, etc., will dry fastest. Remove them from the stalks before drying them or they will be overdone, losing flavor and quality. In very warm areas, they might even scorch. If they do, they will taste just like burned food when you rehydrate them.

13. Dense food like carrots will feel very hard when they are ready. Others will be crispy. Usually, a food that is high in fructose (sugar) will be leathery when it is finished dehydrating.

14. Remember that food smells when it is in the process of drying, so outdoors or in the garage is an excellent place to dry a big batch of those onions!

15. Always test each batch to make sure it is "done."

16. You can pasteurize finished food by putting it in a slow oven (150 degrees F.) for a few minutes.

17. Let the food cool before storing.

18. Store in airtight containers to guard against moisture. Jars saved from other food work well as long as they have lids that will keep moisture out.

19. Zip-closure food storage bags work well.

20. Jars of dehydrated carrots, celery, beets, etc., may look cheerful on your countertop, but the colors and flavors will fade. Dehydrated food keeps its color and flavor best if stored in a dark, cool place.

21. Dehydrating food takes time, so do not rush it. When you are all done, you will have a dried food stash to be proud of!

Freezing

1. Wash all containers and lids in hot, soapy water using soft cloth.
2. Rinse well in clear, clean, hot water.
3. Cool and drain well.
4. Place food into container to within 1 inch of rim. This allows for expansion of food during freezing.
5. Wipe rim of container with clean damp cloth, checking for chips or breaks.
6. Be certain cover fits the container snugly to avoid leaks. Burp air from container.
7. If food is hot when placing in container, cool prior to placing in freezer.
8. Label and date each container.
9. Store upright in freezer until frozen solid.

Pumpkin Leather

This makes a delicious fruit leather full of vitamins.

Ingredients:

pumpkin
honey to taste
spices to taste

Directions:

1. Wash pumpkin, remove seeds, cut into 1-inch-wide slices, and peel.
2. Cut flesh into 1-inch cubes.
3. Cook in water until soft then purée and strain.
4. Add honey and spices to taste.
5. Dry on home food dehydrator tray.
6. Or, cover cookie sheet with plastic wrap and secure with tape.
7. Spread mixture onto plastic wrap in a very thin layer, about ⅛ inch or less.
8. Place in oven at 150 degrees F. with door ajar for about 2 hours or until leather is no longer sticky.
9. Remove from oven and roll up into a log; cut into individual rolls.
10. Store in airtight container in cool place.

Bread and Butter Pickles

My aunt used to make bread and butter pickles, and we all loved them. They make a great addition to your Thanksgiving meal.

Ingredients:

> 12 med. cucumbers, sliced, not peeled
> 6   onions, sliced
> ½   c. salt
> 1   pt. vinegar
> 2   c. sugar
> 1   tsp. ground ginger
> 2   tsp. celery seed
> 1   tsp. turmeric

Directions:

1. Sprinkle cucumbers and onions with salt; let stand ½ hour then rinse with cold water.
2. In large saucepan mix together vinegar, sugar, ginger, celery seed, and turmeric.
3. Add cucumbers and onions, and cook 5 minutes or until yellow.
4. Fill jars, leaving ½-inch headspace.
5. Process in boiling water bath for 5 minutes following basic canning directions found on page 238.

Did You Know? . . . .

Did you know that in the Midwestern United States in the mid to late 1800s, domestic turkeys were actually herded across the range in a manner similar to herding cattle?

Dried Cranberries

My children love dried cranberries, and we all enjoy them in salads.

Ingredients:

- 1 bag fresh whole cranberries (12 oz.)
- 1 c. confectioners' sugar
- ½ c. water

Directions:

1. Preheat oven to 200 degrees F.
2. Put cranberries in large skillet; pick through to remove soft and/or brown berries.
3. Dissolve sugar in water.
4. Pour over cranberries and stir.
5. Heat on medium-high until cranberries pop, 4 to 5 minutes or so, stirring every minute or two.
6. When all seem popped, turn off heat and let cool for 10 minutes.
7. Squash cranberries with back of large spoon. (Do not worry if they seem to be melding together.)
8. Let cool another 5 minutes.
9. Cover baking sheet with three layers of paper towels and a piece of parchment paper.
10. Spread cranberries on parchment.
11. If unpopped ones remain, squash them. (As they dry, berries will separate again.)
12. Place in oven and turn heat down to 150 degrees F. (or follow directions for your food dehydrator).
13. In 2 to 4 hours, replace parchment and flip paper towels over. (This step will speed up drying process.)
14. Start checking after 6 hours. (Total time depends on humidity and whether you want some give in them or whether you like them crispier.)
15. Separate berries and store covered.

Fruit Leather

My children love fruit leather, and it is always best homemade.

Ingredients:

½ c. sugar
  apples, apricots, pears, peaches, strawberries, etc.

Directions:

1. Wash and pit or remove seeds; chop and then cook pulp.
2. Place 1 cup of pulp at a time in blender and purée.
3. Combine pulp and sugar.
4. Cover cookie sheet with plastic wrap and secure with tape.
5. Spread mixture onto plastic wrap in a very thin layer, about ⅛ inch or less.
6. Place in oven at 150 degrees with door ajar for about 2 hours or until leather is no longer sticky (or follow directions for your food dehydrator).
7. Remove from oven and roll up into a log; cut into individual rolls.
8. Store in airtight container in cool place.

Did You Know? . . . .

Did you know that in the Middle Ages stuffing was known as farce, from the Latin farcire, which means to stuff? The term "stuffing" first appears in English print in 1538. After about 1880, the term "stuffing" was replaced by "dressing" in Victorian English.

Pickled Pumpkin

Double or triple this recipe and use up those Halloween pumpkins. The longer the pickled pumpkin is stored before serving, the better it tastes.

Ingredients:

    4 lb. pumpkin, peeled, diced
    5 c. sugar
    5 c. white vinegar
    4 cinnamon sticks
    15 whole cloves

Directions:

1. Place pumpkin in large, deep bowl.
2. In large saucepan mix sugar, vinegar, cinnamon sticks, and cloves; boil 5 minutes.
3. Pour hot liquid over pumpkin.
4. Cover and set aside 8 hours or overnight.
5. Strain liquid into large saucepan.
6. Bring to a boil and boil 5 minutes.
7. Remove cinnamon sticks and cloves, leaving a few bits for decoration.
8. Place pumpkin back into liquid and return to boiling.
9. Boil 5 minutes or until pumpkin is transparent but crisp.
10. Allow mixture to cool.
11. Transfer to sterile jars, seal, and refrigerate.

Yields: 16 cups.

***Did You Know?* . . . .**

Did you know that gourds are from the same family as squashes?

Preserving Winter Squash or Pumpkin

Sixteen pounds of cubed winter squash or pumpkin will make seven quarts of canned squash. This is great to have on hand to pull out for a pie.

Directions for canning:

1. Wash squash, remove seeds, cut into 1-inch-wide slices, and peel.
2. Cut flesh into 1-inch cubes.
3. Boil 2 minutes in water. (Do not mash or purée.)
4. Fill jars with cubes and cooking liquid, leaving 1-inch headspace.
5. Adjust lids.
6. Process in dial-gauge pressure canner at 11 pounds pressure or in a weighted-gauge pressure canner at 10 pounds pressure (15 pounds if above 1000 feet altitude)—Pints: 55 minutes; Quarts: 90 minutes.
7. For making pies, drain jars and strain or sieve cubes.

Directions for freezing:

1. Wash squash, remove seeds, cut into 1-inch-wide slices, and peel.
2. Cut flesh into 1-inch cubes.
3. Cook in water until soft, then mash.
4. Pack into containers leaving ½-inch headspace.
5. Freeze.

Directions for drying:

1. Wash, peel, and remove fibers and seeds from flesh.
2. Cut into small, thin strips.
3. Blanch strips over steam for 5 to 6 minutes and cool rapidly.
4. Dry strips in dehydrator until brittle.
5. Store in dry, cold area for longest shelf life. (Freezer storage is ideal.)
6. If rehydrated, dried pumpkin can be puréed in blender and used for pies or baby food.
7. Dried pumpkin can also be ground into "flour."

Pumpkin Seeds

Our family loves eating pumpkin seeds, and these are delicious. Season to your own personal taste.

Ingredients:

    2   qt. water
    ¼   c. salt
    1-2 Tbs. melted butter or oil
    1   tsp. garlic or onion salt
         pumpkin seeds

Directions:

1. Scoop seeds from pumpkin and, without washing, spread them out to dry.
2. Pumpkin seeds can be dried at room temperature, in a dehydrator at 115 to 120 degrees F. for 1 to 2 hours, or in a warm oven for 3 to 4 hours.
3. If drying in oven, stir frequently to avoid scorching.
4. When dry, separate fiber from seeds.
5. In colander, rinse seeds thoroughly with water.
6. Dry seeds on absorbent paper.
7. In large saucepan, put 2 quarts water and the salt; add seeds.
8. Bring to a boil and simmer about 2 hours (seeds will turn gray).
9. Drain seeds and dry well on absorbent paper.
10. In bowl mix 2 cups seeds with 1 to 2 tablespoons melted butter or oil; sprinkle with 1 teaspoon garlic or onion salt, or experiment with your family's favorite spice or flavoring.
11. To roast, preheat oven to 250 degrees F.
12. Spread seeds in shallow baking pan, and roast in oven, stirring occasionally, until lightly browned and crisp, about 20 to 30 minutes.
13. Cool and seal in airtight container for 1 to 2 weeks.
14. For longer storage, seeds may be frozen.

Sweet Pickled Pears

This recipe can be used for peaches, too.

Ingredients:

6-7 lb. pears
2   lb. brown sugar
2   c. cider vinegar
1   oz. stick cinnamon
    whole cloves

Directions:

1. Wash pears.
2. If using small, hard pears such as Seckels, do not pare; pare only if skins are tough.
3. Large pears may be quartered.
4. Stick each pear with 3 cloves.
5. In saucepan stir together sugar, vinegar, and cinnamon, and boil for 20 minutes.
6. Add pears one half at a time, and cook in syrup only until tender when pricked with a fork.
7. Fill hot sterilized jars with fruit, add hot syrup, and seal, following basic canning directions found on page 238.
8. For peaches: Dip peaches briefly in hot water, then rub off fuzz with a towel.
9. Stick each peach with 4 cloves instead of 3, and proceed with recipe.

Yields: 3 to 4 quarts.

***Did You Know?* . . . .**

Did you know that American Revolutionary War veteran Henry Hall is alleged to be the first to cultivate the cranberry commercially around 1816?

Sweet Pickles

My aunt used to make sweet pickles that I enjoyed as a child.

Ingredients:

9-15 med. cucumbers (about 4½ inches long)
6   c. boiling water
2⅓   c. white vinegar
1¼   c. sugar
3   Tbs. pickling salt
1   Tbs. celery seeds
3¼   tsp. turmeric
¾   tsp. mustard seeds

Directions:

1. Select fresh, firm cucumbers.
2. Wash and cut into spears.
3. Pour boiling water over spears and let stand overnight.
4. The next day, drain cucumbers and pack solidly into hot, sterilized pint jars.
5. Combine remaining ingredients and boil 5 minutes.
6. Pour syrup over cucumbers, leaving ½-inch headspace.
7. Adjust lids.
8. Process in boiling water bath canner for 5 minutes. (See directions on page 238.)
9. Remove to towel to cool completely.
10. After jars cool, check seals.
11. Store in cool, dark place.

Yields: 3 pints.

Turkey Jerky

Our family and children love turkey jerky. It is easy to make in your dehydrator or oven. Turkey does not take as long to dehydrate as beef, so keep an eye on it. Adjust seasonings to your taste.

Ingredients:

- 1 lb. turkey breast
- 4 Tbs. soy sauce or tamari soy sauce
- 1 tsp. lemon juice
- 1 tsp. lime juice
- 1 tsp. brown sugar
- ½ tsp. black pepper
- ½ tsp. cayenne pepper
- ¼ tsp. ground allspice
- ¼ tsp. garlic powder

Directions:

1. Slice turkey breast about ⅛ to ¼ inch thick and cut into strips.
2. Combine marinade ingredients in resealable plastic food storage bag.
3. Add turkey strips and turn to coat evenly.
4. Press out any air from bag and seal closed.
5. Refrigerate for 24 hours, picking up bag once or twice during that time to redistribute marinade.
6. If using a dehydrator, follow manufacturer's instructions.
7. Preheat oven to 250 degrees F.
8. Remove turkey strips from marinade, drain well, and lay on wire rack placed on top of baking sheet lined with aluminum foil.
9. Bake strips, turning once, until brown and leathery, 3½ to 4 hours.
10. Let cool completely, then place in a resealable food storage bag or tightly capped jar.

Thanksgiving Delights Cookbook

A Collection of Thanksgiving Recipes
Cookbook Delights Holiday Series Book 11

Salads

Table of Contents

Did You Know? . . . .

Did you know that cranberries are a major commercial crop in certain U.S. states and Canadian provinces?

Cabbage Salad

My family likes two different versions of cabbage for the holidays, so we make one head with vinegar and oil dressing and one head with creamy mayonnaise-mustard dressing.

Ingredients for vinegar and oil style:

- 1   head green cabbage, thickly shredded
- ¼   c. balsamic vinegar
- ¼   c. extra-virgin olive oil
- salt and pepper to taste

Directions for vinegar and oil style:

1. Shortly before serving, mix together vinegar, olive oil, and salt and pepper.
2. Toss dressing with cabbage.
3. Adjust seasonings.
4. Serve or chill.

Ingredients for creamy mayonnaise-mustard style:

- 1   head green cabbage, thickly shredded
- ¾   c. mayonnaise
- ¼   c. prepared mustard
- 1   Tbs. Worcestershire sauce
- ¼   tsp. garlic salt
- ¼   tsp. pepper

Directions for creamy mayonnaise-mustard style:

1. Shortly before serving, mix together dressing ingredients.
2. Toss dressing with cabbage.
3. Adjust seasonings.
4. Serve or chill.

Chinese Turkey Pasta Salad

This is an interesting way to serve turkey salad.

Ingredients:

2	c. uncooked spiral pasta
2	c. cubed cooked turkey
1½	c. snow peas, fresh or frozen, thawed
½	c. chopped sweet red pepper
½	c. chopped green pepper
¼	c. thinly sliced green onions
¼	c. diced celery
1	can sliced water chestnuts (8 oz.), drained
1	jar diced pimientos (2 oz.), drained
1	c. mayonnaise
2	Tbs. soy sauce
1	tsp. sugar
1	tsp. ground ginger
¼-½	tsp. hot pepper sauce
1	c. salted cashew halves, divided

Directions:

1. Cook pasta according to package directions; drain and rinse in cold water.
2. Place in large bowl; add turkey and vegetables.
3. In small bowl combine mayonnaise, soy sauce, sugar, ginger, and hot pepper sauce.
4. Stir in ½ cup cashews.
5. Pour over pasta mixture and toss to coat.
6. Cover and refrigerate for at least 1 hour before serving.
7. Sprinkle with remaining cashews just before serving.

Yields: 4 to 6 servings.

Cranberry Fruit Salad

This makes a colorful and festive holiday fruit salad.

Ingredients:

- 1½ c. water
- 1½ c. sugar
- 12 oz. fresh cranberries
- 1½ c. Navel oranges, peeled, cubed
- ½ c. red apple, cored, cubed
- ½ c. banana, peeled, sliced
- 2 Tbs. chopped pecans

Directions:

1. In medium saucepan combine water, sugar, and cranberries.
2. Cook over medium heat until cranberries just begin to open, stirring occasionally.
3. Transfer cranberries to large bowl.
4. Cover bowl and refrigerate at least 2 hours.
5. Fold in oranges, apple, banana, and pecans.
6. Cover and refrigerate at least 1 hour.

Gorgonzola Salad

Gorgonzola adds great flavor to salad greens.

Ingredients:

- 12 c. mixed baby greens
- 2 green onions, sliced
- ½ c. crumbled Gorgonzola cheese (about 2½ oz.)
- ½ c. chopped walnuts, toasted
  ranch dressing
  Blue Cheese Dressing (recipe page 173)
  Balsamic Vinaigrette (recipe page 168)

Directions:

1. Rinse and drain greens.
2. Combine mixed greens and green onions in large bowl.
3. Sprinkle cheese and walnuts over top.
4. Serve with ranch or blue cheese dressings or balsamic vinaigrette.

Yields: About 6 servings.

Cranberry Fluff

This fluffy fruit salad gets its sweet-tart flavor from cranberries and whipped cream.

Ingredients:

4   c. cranberries, fresh or frozen
3   c. miniature marshmallows
¾   c. sugar
2   c. unpeeled, diced tart apples
½   c. green grapes, halved
½   c. chopped walnuts
¼   tsp. salt
1   c. whipping cream, whipped

Directions:

1. Place cranberries in food processor or blender; cover and process until finely chopped.
2. Transfer to a bowl; add marshmallows and sugar.
3. Cover and refrigerate for 4 hours or overnight.
4. Just before serving, stir in apples, grapes, walnuts, and salt.
5. Fold in whipped cream.

Yields: 10 to 12 servings.

Cranberry Waldorf Salad

This is a colorful holiday salad.

Ingredients for dressing:

    2   eggs
    ⅓   c. sugar
    ¼   c. orange juice
    2   Tbs. water
    2   Tbs. grated orange peel

Ingredients for salad:

    2   c. cranberries, fresh or frozen
    2   med. oranges, peeled, chopped (about 1 c.) or 1 can
        mandarin oranges, drained
    1   lg. apple, chopped (about 1 c.)
    1   c. chopped dates
    ⅓   c. chopped walnuts
    2   c. miniature marshmallows

Directions for dressing:

1. In 4-cup measure beat eggs well with whisk.
2. Add remaining dressing ingredients.
3. Beat with whisk until mixture is smooth.
4. Microwave at 50% (medium) for 4 to 6 minutes or until mixture thickens, beating with whisk every 2 minutes.
5. Chill about 2 hours or until cold.

Directions for salad:

1. In large mixing bowl combine salad ingredients.
2. Spoon dressing over salad.
3. Toss gently to coat.

Yields: 10 to 12 servings.

Cranbrosia

This in an interesting variation of the classic ambrosia.

Ingredients:

- 1   can mandarin oranges (11 oz.)
- 1   can pineapple chunks (8 oz.)
- 2   env. unflavored gelatin
- 2   c. fresh cranberries
- 1   c. sugar
- 1   c. sweetened flaked coconut
- 8   oz. sour cream (1 c.)
- 1   c. whipping cream
- 1   banana, sliced

Directions:

1. Drain mandarin oranges and pineapple, reserving juices separately; set fruit aside.
2. Sprinkle gelatin over reserved mandarin orange juice in small saucepan; let stand 1 minute.
3. Cook over low heat, stirring until gelatin dissolves.
4. Stir in reserved pineapple juice; set aside.
5. Using food processor, finely chop cranberries.
6. Place chopped cranberries in large bowl.
7. Add reserved gelatin mixture, sugar, and remaining ingredients; stir well.
8. Spoon mixture into 7-cup mold; cover and chill 8 hours.
9. To serve, unmold onto serving plate.

Yields: 10 servings.

Did You Know? . . . .

Did you know that Wisconsin is the leading producer of cranberries, with nearly half of U.S. production?

Gingered Apple Slaw

This is a refreshing, crunchy salad.

Ingredients:

⅓ lb. Granny Smith apples
½ lb. Golden Delicious apples
⅓ lb. red apples
4 oz. celery
½ c. mayonnaise
1½ tsp. grated fresh ginger
1 Tbs. seasoned rice vinegar

Directions:

1. Cut apples and celery into matchsticks.
2. Combine mayonnaise, ginger, and vinegar; mix well.
3. Add apple and celery sticks and toss gently.

Yields: 6 servings.

Creamy Sweet Potato Salad

This makes a great salad. Be sure not to overcook the sweet potatoes.

Ingredients:

2 c. mayonnaise
⅓ c. buttermilk
2 Tbs. lemon juice
1 Tbs. Dijon mustard
1 tsp. sugar
3 lb. sweet potatoes, cooked but firm, peeled, cubed
1 c. peas
½ c. sweet red pepper, chunked
½ c. green onions, sliced
1 bunch fresh spinach
3 strips bacon, cooked, crumbled

Directions:

1. In bowl blend mayonnaise, buttermilk, lemon juice, mustard, and sugar until smooth.
2. In large bowl combine sweet potatoes, peas, pepper, and onions.
3. Pour dressing over all and toss to blend.
4. Chill at least two hours or overnight.
5. To serve, spoon salad into large bowl lined with spinach, and top with crumbled bacon.

Sweet Potato Slaw

The sweet potatoes look like carrots in this distinctive salad.

Ingredients:

½ c. mayonnaise
½ c. sour cream
2 Tbs. honey
2 Tbs. lemon juice
1 tsp. grated lemon peel
½ tsp. salt
¼ tsp. pepper
3 c. peeled, shredded, uncooked sweet potatoes
1 med. apple, peeled, chopped
1 can pineapple tidbits (8 oz.), drained
½ c. chopped pecans

Directions:

1. In bowl combine first 7 ingredients; blend until smooth.
2. In large bowl combine potatoes, apple, pineapple, and pecans.
3. Add dressing and toss to coat.
4. Cover and refrigerate at least 1 hour.

Yields: 6 to 8 servings.

Cranberry Couscous Salad

This satisfying salad has an interesting mix of good-for-you ingredients.

Ingredients:

1   c. water
¾   c. uncooked couscous
¾   c. dried cranberries
½   c. chopped carrots
½   c. chopped, seeded cucumber
¼   c. thinly sliced green onions
3   Tbs. balsamic vinegar
1   Tbs. olive oil
2   tsp. Dijon mustard
½   tsp. salt
⅛   tsp. pepper
¼   c. slivered almonds, toasted

Directions:

1. In saucepan bring water to a boil; stir in couscous.
2. Remove from heat; cover and let stand for 5 minutes.
3. Fluff with a fork and cool for 10 minutes.
4. In bowl combine couscous, cranberries, carrots, cucumber, and green onions.
5. In small bowl combine vinegar, oil, mustard, salt, and pepper.
6. Pour over couscous mixture; mix well.
7. Cover and refrigerate.
8. Just before serving, stir in almonds.

Yields: 6 servings.

Greens with Pears and Pecans

Pears and blue cheese are a great contrast in flavor.

Ingredients:

- ½ c. pecan halves
- 2 Tbs. cider vinegar
- 1 Tbs. chopped shallots
- 7 Tbs. extra-virgin olive oil
- 1 qt. baby salad greens, washed, dried
- 4 Seckel pears, quartered, cored, sliced
- ⅓ lb. blue cheese (preferably made with buttermilk)
  salt and freshly ground pepper to taste

Directions:

1. Preheat oven to 350 degrees F.
2. Spread pecans on baking sheet and toast in oven until they smell nutty, 7 to 10 minutes, stirring once or twice as they toast.
3. Transfer pan to wire rack to cool.
4. In small bowl whisk together vinegar, shallots, salt, and pepper.
5. Slowly drizzle in oil, whisking to incorporate.
6. Taste and adjust seasonings.
7. Crumble cheese.
8. In large bowl toss together greens, pears, cheese, and dressing.
9. Taste and add more salt and pepper if necessary.
10. Sprinkle nuts on top and serve immediately.

Yields: 4 servings.

Did You Know? . . . .

Did you know that in 2003 the two turkeys pardoned by the President were named Stars and Stripes?

Spinach Salad with Red Potatoes

This salad is hearty and flavorful.

Ingredients:

- 1 pkg. fresh spinach (10 oz.), torn
- 3 sm. red potatoes, cooked, diced
- 2 hard-boiled eggs, chopped
- ½ c. sliced fresh mushrooms
- 4 bacon strips, diced
- ¼ c. chopped red onion
- ½ tsp. cornstarch
- ¼ c. apple juice
- 2 Tbs. cider vinegar
- 2 tsp. sugar
- ⅛ tsp. pepper

Directions:

1. In salad bowl combine spinach, potatoes, eggs, and mushrooms.
2. In skillet cook bacon until crisp.
3. Remove bacon with slotted spoon; drain on paper towels.
4. Sauté onion in bacon drippings until tender.
5. Combine cornstarch, apple juice, vinegar, sugar, and pepper until smooth; stir into skillet.
6. Bring to a boil; cook and stir for 1 to 2 minutes or until slightly thickened and bubbly.
7. Pour over spinach mixture.
8. Add bacon and toss.
9. Serve immediately.

Yields: 8 servings.

Strawberry Pretzel Salad

This is one of my children's favorites. It can be served as a salad or dessert.

Ingredients:

2 c. crushed hard pretzels
¾ c. melted butter
1 c. plus 3 Tbs. sugar, divided
8 oz. cream cheese, softened
2 c. Sweetened Whipped Cream (recipe page 157)
1 pkg. strawberry gelatin (6 oz.)
2 c. boiling water
1 pkg. frozen strawberries (10 oz.)
 fresh strawberries for garnish

Directions:

1. Preheat oven to 400 degrees F.
2. Mix together crushed pretzels, butter, and 3 tablespoons sugar.
3. Press into bottom of 13 x 9 x 2-inch baking dish; bake for 8 to 10 minutes or until lightly toasted.
4. Set aside to cool completely.
5. In medium bowl beat cream cheese and 1 cup sugar until smooth.
6. Fold in whipped cream.
7. Spread evenly over cooled crust; refrigerate until set, about 30 minutes.
8. In medium bowl stir gelatin into boiling water.
9. Mix in frozen strawberries; stir until thawed.
10. Spoon over cream cheese mixture.
11. Refrigerate until completely chilled, at least 1 hour.
12. Garnish with fresh strawberries.

Yields: 12 servings.

Marinated Tomatoes with Mozzarella Balls in Balsamic Vinegar

Fresh mozzarella balls are delicious with balsamic vinegar reduction. This is one of our favorite salads.

Ingredients:

7	lg. tomatoes
1½	lb. cherry-size fresh mozzarella balls
1	c. olive oil
1½	c. balsamic vinegar, boiled, reduced to ¾ c.
1	Tbs. salt
¾	tsp. freshly ground pepper
2	cloves garlic, crushed
3	Tbs. chopped fresh parsley
3	Tbs. chopped fresh basil (or 1 Tbs. dried basil)
½	c. chopped onion

Directions:

1. Cut tomatoes into ½-inch-thick slices and arrange in large, shallow dish.
2. Add mozzarella balls; set aside.
3. Combine remaining ingredients in jar.
4. Cover tightly and shake vigorously.
5. Pour over tomato slices and cheese balls.
6. Cover and marinate in refrigerator several hours.

Yields: 20 servings.

Did You Know? . . . .

Did you know that when eaten at Christmas in Britain, turkey is traditionally served with winter vegetables, including roast potatoes, Brussels sprouts, and parsnips?

Thanksgiving Delights Cookbook

A Collection of Thanksgiving Recipes
Cookbook Delights Holiday Series Book 11

Side Dishes

Table of Contents

Did You Know? . . . .

Did you know that in North America, Native Americans were the first to recognize and use the cranberry as a source of food?

Apricot Cranberry Stuffing

There are so many different kinds of stuffing. It is fun to keep trying the many variations.

Ingredients:

- 1 loaf whole-wheat bread
- 1 lg. onion, finely chopped
- ½ c. chopped celery
- 1 c. apple, peeled, chopped
- ¾ c. dried apricots, chopped
- ½ c. dried cranberries
- 1 lg. zucchini, grated
- 2 eggs
- ½ c. olive oil
- 6 sprigs fresh thyme
  salt and pepper to taste

Directions:

1. Preheat oven to 325 degrees F.
2. Crumble or cube bread; place in large bowl.
3. Add remaining ingredients; mix well. (Mixture should be moist and sticking together.)
4. Put stuffing into foil loaf pan.
5. Cover with foil (may refrigerate for up to 8 hours).
6. Bake, covered, for 1 hour.
7. If drier stuffing is desired, uncover and bake another 10 to 15 minutes.

Did You Know? . . . .

Did you know that about 95 percent of cranberries are processed into products such as juice drinks, sauce, and sweetened dried cranberries? The remaining 5 percent are sold fresh to consumers.

Candied Yams

This makes a great side dish for Thanksgiving dinner.

Ingredients:

    4   med. yams, peeled, cut into 1-inch slices
    ½   tsp. salt
    4   Tbs. butter
    1   c. sugar
    ¾   c. chopped pecans
    ½   tsp. ground cinnamon
    ¼   tsp. ground cloves
    ¼   tsp. ground nutmeg
    4   c. miniature marshmallows

Directions:

1. Preheat oven to 375 degrees F.
2. Butter 13 x 9 x 2-inch baking dish.
3. In medium saucepan cover yams with water; add salt.
4. Boil until tender but firm; drain.
5. In prepared baking dish layer ingredients and sprinkle with spices.
6. Bake until golden, about 30 minutes.
7. Remove from oven and top with marshmallows.
8. Continue to bake until marshmallows are lightly browned and melted; do not allow to burn.

Yields: 6 to 8 servings.

Did You Know? . . . .

Did you know that 1934 was the first year a Mickey Mouse balloon was entered in the Macy's Thanksgiving Day Parade?

Celery Dressing

This is an excellent stuffing. I toast our favorite whole-wheat bread to add flavor to the bread cubes.

Ingredients:

1   c. butter
1   c. minced onion
4   c. diced celery, with leaves
6   c. chicken broth
8   qt. whole-wheat bread cubes
6   eggs
1   Tbs. salt
2   tsp. ground black pepper
½   tsp. sage
1   pinch dried thyme
1   pinch dried marjoram

Directions:

1. Preheat oven to 350 degrees F.
2. Melt butter in saucepan.
3. Sauté onion in butter until soft but not brown.
4. Add celery and stir well.
5. Add 2 cups broth and bring to a boil.
6. Cover and simmer 10 minutes.
7. Place bread cubes in large mixing bowl.
8. Add eggs, salt, pepper, sage, thyme, and marjoram.
9. Add onion and celery mixture; combine thoroughly.
10. If still too dry, add more chicken broth.
11. Place in buttered baking dish, and bake for 45 minutes or until top is lightly browned.
12. More broth may be needed for this method to keep it from drying out.

Yields: 32 cups.

Chestnut Dressing

Chestnuts add delicious flavor and texture to this dressing.

Ingredients:

- 2 Tbs. butter
- 1 c. chopped celery
- ⅓ c. chopped onion
- 8 c. toasted whole-wheat bread crumbs
- 2 c. boiled chestnuts, shelled, chopped
- 2 tsp. salt
- ½ tsp. pepper
- ½ tsp. dried basil
- ½ tsp. dried sage
- ½ tsp. dried marjoram
- ½ tsp. dried rosemary
- ½ tsp. dried thyme
- ⅔ c. butter, melted
  broth or water to moisten

Directions:

1. Preheat oven to 350 degrees F.
2. Sauté celery and onion in 2 tablespoons butter until tender.
3. Combine bread crumbs, chestnuts, sautéed celery and onion, and seasonings.
4. Add butter and enough liquid to moisten.
5. Toss gently to mix.
6. Transfer to oiled large casserole dish; cover and bake 30 minutes.
7. Uncover and bake 20 minutes more.

Cornbread Dressing

This old-fashioned cornbread dressing is flavorful, tender, and moist.

Ingredients for cornbread:

3	Tbs. bacon drippings
2	lg. eggs
1½	c. cornmeal
1	tsp. salt
½	tsp. baking soda
1	tsp. baking powder
1¼	c. buttermilk

Ingredients for dressing:

1	pan cornbread (13 x 9-in.), crumbled (recipe above)
10	white or whole-wheat bread heels (left out overnight)
3	lg. stalks celery, chopped
1	lg. onion, chopped (2½ to 3 c.)
1	lg. green pepper, chopped
¾	c. butter
¼	lb. bacon, fried crisp, crumbled
3	lg. eggs, slightly beaten
4	c. chicken stock
1	c. turkey pan drippings
2	tsp. poultry seasoning (recipe page 178)
½	tsp. rubbed sage
½	tsp. freshly ground black pepper

Directions for cornbread:

1. Preheat oven to 450 degrees F.
2. Put bacon drippings in 13 x 9 x 2-inch baking dish and place in oven while it is preheating to melt drippings.

3. Beat eggs in medium bowl until frothy.
4. Add cornmeal, salt, soda, and baking powder; stir to combine.
5. Add buttermilk and stir well.
6. Remove hot dish from oven; swirl dish to coat with melted bacon drippings.
7. Pour bacon drippings into batter; stir to combine.
8. Pour batter into pan, and bake for 20 to 25 minutes. (Cornbread will begin to pull away from sides of dish.)
9. Note: Make cornbread a day before you intend to make dressing. Leave it out uncovered overnight.

Directions for dressing:

1. Preheat oven to 375 degrees F.
2. Crumble cornbread and white bread into very large baking dish or pan. (This is the pan dressing will be cooked in, and room is needed to stir it while it is cooking.)
3. In large skillet sauté celery, onion, and green pepper in butter over medium heat until onion is transparent.
4. Combine sautéed vegetables and bacon with bread crumbs and mix well.
5. Note: Dressing can be prepared up to this point an hour or so in advance.
6. When ready to bake dressing, add beaten eggs, chicken stock, and turkey pan drippings; stir.
7. Use additional chicken stock if needed.
8. Add poultry seasoning, sage, and pepper; mix thoroughly.
9. After baking for 15 minutes, stir dressing down from sides of pan so it cooks uniformly.
10. Check seasonings; if more sage is needed, add ¼ teaspoon or so with a little chicken stock, stir in, and taste again.
11. Total cooking time should be about 30 minutes.

Giblet Dressing

My mom and aunts used to make giblet dressing.

Ingredients:

1   lb. turkey giblets
¼   tsp. salt
½   c. butter
½   c. chopped onion
¼   c. finely chopped celery
8   c. toasted whole-wheat bread crumbs (about 14
    slices of bread)
4   hard-boiled eggs, chopped
1   tsp. seasoned salt (recipe page 180)
¼   tsp. dried rosemary
¼   tsp. dried sage
¼   tsp. dried thyme
¼   tsp. dried marjoram
¼   tsp. pepper

Directions:

1. In saucepan combine giblets (except the liver),
   enough water to cover, and salt.
2. Cover and simmer for about 2 hours, until tender.
3. Add liver; cover and simmer for 25 minutes longer.
4. Cool giblets and broth slightly.
5. Preheat oven to 350 degrees F.
6. Remove and chop giblets; set aside and reserve 1 cup
   of broth.
7. Melt butter in skillet over medium-low heat.
8. Add onion and celery; cook until tender.
9. Combine with bread crumbs, chopped eggs, chopped
   giblets, seasoned salt, seasonings, and pepper.
10. Add reserved broth, tossing lightly to moisten.
11. Spoon into buttered 2-quart baking dish.
12. Cover tightly and bake for 40 to 45 minutes.

Glazed Sweet Potatoes with Apples and Pecans

The combination of apples and sweet potatoes in this sweet and savory dish is perfect for a Thanksgiving dinner. Pecans give it a delicious crunch.

Ingredients:

- 6 med. sweet potatoes, peeled, sliced ¼ inch thick
- 1 tsp. salt
- 2 med. apples, peeled, cored, sliced ¼ inch thick
- 4 Tbs. butter
- ¼ tsp. ground nutmeg
- ½ c. maple syrup
- ½ c. apple cider
- ½ c. coarsely chopped pecans

Directions:

1. Preheat oven to 400 degrees F.
2. Bring 3 quarts water to a boil in large saucepan; add sweet potatoes and salt.
3. Boil for 6 to 7 minutes or until just tender; remove from heat.
4. With slotted spoon, transfer potatoes to 13 x 9 x 2-inch baking dish coated with nonstick cooking spray.
5. Add apple slices; stir to combine.
6. In small saucepan combine butter, nutmeg, maple syrup, and apple cider over medium heat.
7. Stir and bring just to a boil; remove from heat.
8. Pour over sweet potato mixture and scatter with pecans.
9. Bake for 25 to 30 minutes or until glaze thickens, sweet potatoes and apples are tender, and pecans turn light brown.

Yields: 12 servings.

Orange-Buttered Peas

Orange adds a delightful flavor to the peas.

Ingredients:

- 3 Tbs. Orange Marmalade (recipe page 192)
- 2 Tbs. butter
- 1 Tbs. grated orange peel
- ½ c. sliced fresh mushrooms
- 1 pkg. frozen peas (16 oz.)
  salt and pepper to taste

Directions:

1. In saucepan over medium heat, combine marmalade, butter, and orange peel.
2. Add mushrooms; cook and stir until tender.
3. Cook peas according to package directions; drain.
4. Add mushroom mixture and toss.
5. Season with salt and pepper.

Yields: 6 to 8 servings.

Baked Corn Pudding

This is a traditional Thanksgiving side dish.

Ingredients:

- 2 pkg. frozen corn (10 oz. each)
- 3 eggs, well beaten
- 1 tsp. grated onion
- ¼ c. all-purpose flour
- 2 tsp. salt
- ¼ tsp. white pepper
- 1 Tbs. sugar
- 1 dash ground nutmeg
- 2 Tbs. butter

2   c. light cream
1   can pimientos (4 oz.)

Directions:

1. Preheat oven to 325 degrees F.
2. Lightly grease 1½-quart shallow baking dish.
3. Combine all ingredients in large bowl; mix well.
4. Transfer to greased baking dish, and bake 1 hour or until pudding is firm or knife comes out clean.
5. Serve hot.

Butternut Squash and Apples

This makes a pleasant side dish for your Thanksgiving meal.

Ingredients:

3   lb. butternut squash
3   baking apples
6   Tbs. butter, softened
⅔   c. brown sugar, firmly packed
1½ Tbs. all-purpose flour
1¼ tsp. salt

Directions:

1. Preheat oven to 350 degrees F.
2. Cut squash in halves; remove seeds and fiber.
3. Peel and cut in slices ½ to ¾ inch thick.
4. Arrange in 13 x 9 x 2-inch baking pan.
5. Core apples but do not peel.
6. Cut in ½- to ¾-inch slices; lay on top squash.
7. Mix butter, brown sugar, flour, and salt.
8. Sprinkle over top of apples and squash.
9. Cover pan tightly with aluminum foil.
10. Bake about 1 hour, until squash is tender.

Yields: About 9 servings.

Sausage, Apple, and Cranberry Stuffing

This Thanksgiving stuffing is very flavorful and fresh-tasting. This recipe will stuff a ten-pound turkey. Make sure you follow turkey and stuffing directions when you prepare these recipes.

Ingredients:

2½ c. cubed whole-wheat bread
2¾ c. cubed white bread
1 lb. ground turkey sausage
1 c. chopped onion
1 c. chopped celery
2½ tsp. dried sage
1½ tsp. dried rosemary
½ tsp. dried thyme
1 Golden Delicious apple, cored, chopped
¾ c. dried cranberries
⅓ c. minced fresh parsley
¾ c. turkey stock
4 Tbs. unsalted butter, melted

Directions:

1. Preheat oven to 350 degrees F.
2. Spread white and whole-wheat bread cubes in single layer on large baking sheet.
3. Bake for 5 to 7 minutes or until evenly toasted.
4. Transfer to large bowl.
5. In large skillet cook sausage and onions over medium heat, stirring and breaking up lumps until evenly browned.
6. Add celery, sage, rosemary, and thyme; cook and stir for 2 minutes to blend flavors.
7. Pour sausage mixture over bread in bowl.
8. Mix in chopped apples, dried cranberries, and parsley.
9. Drizzle with turkey stock and melted butter; mix lightly.

10. Transfer mixture to greased 13 x 9 x 2-inch baking dish.
11. Cover and bake for 30 minutes.
12. Uncover and bake 15 to 20 minutes longer or until lightly browned.

Yields: 10 servings.

Roasted Garlic Mashed Potatoes

Our family loves garlic mashed potatoes, and these are delicious.

Ingredients:

    3   lb. red potatoes
    6   cloves garlic
    ½   c. butter
        olive oil
        half-and-half
        salt and pepper to taste
        paprika for garnish

Directions:

1. Peel potatoes, halve, and boil for 25 minutes.
2. Coat garlic skin with olive oil, and bake at 350 degrees F. for 15 minutes; set aside.
3. Drain potatoes.
4. Add butter and enough half-and-half while mashing to get consistency you desire.
5. Squeeze garlic out of skins into potatoes.
6. Add salt and pepper to taste.
7. Transfer to serving bowl and sprinkle top of potatoes with paprika.

Green Bean and French Onion Casserole

This simple dish is always a family favorite.

Ingredients:

2   Tbs. butter
2   Tbs. all-purpose flour
1   tsp. salt
1   tsp. sugar
¼   c. diced onion
1   c. sour cream
4   c. cooked green beans
1⅓ c. French-fried onions, divided

Directions:

1. Preheat oven to 350 degrees F.
2. Melt butter in large skillet over medium heat.
3. Stir in flour until smooth; cook for 1 minute.
4. Stir in salt, sugar, onion, and sour cream.
5. Add green beans and ⅔ c. French-fried onions; stir to coat.
6. Transfer mixture to 2½-qt. casserole dish.
7. Bake for 25 minutes.
8. Top with remaining ⅔ cup French-fried onions.
9. Return to oven and bake 5 minutes more, until onions are lightly browned.

Yields: 6 servings.

Did You Know?....

Did you know that a child born at sea on the Mayflower was named Oceanus?

Thanksgiving Delights Cookbook

A Collection of Thanksgiving Recipes
Cookbook Delights Holiday Series Book 11

Soups

Table of Contents

Did You Know? . . . .

Did you know that according to the USDA, one-sixth of the more than 45 million turkeys that are sold in the U.S. each year are cooked and eaten for Thanksgiving?

Apple Squash Soup

Try this soup recipe that was given to us. My daughter Mikayla enjoys the vegetarian version. Apples and juice add an extra sweetness to the squash in this soup. Ginger and mace partner well with the apples and butternut squash.

Ingredients:

    5   Tbs. unsalted butter
    3   c. chopped onions
    1   tsp. ground ginger
    ½   tsp. ground mace
    3   med. butternut squash (about 4 lb.), peeled, seeded, ½-inch dice
    3   Granny Smith apples, peeled, cored, ½-inch dice
    5   c. chicken or vegetable broth
    2   c. apple juice
    2   Tbs. chopped flat-leaf parsley or finely snipped fresh chives for garnish
        salt and freshly ground pepper to taste

Directions:

1. Melt butter over low heat.
2. Add onions, ginger, and mace; cover and cook, stirring occasionally, until onions are tender, about 15 minutes.
3. Add squash, apples, and broth; bring to a boil.
4. Reduce heat and simmer, partially covered, until squash is tender, about 25 minutes.
5. Strain soup, reserving broth.
6. Purée vegetables in food processor in batches, adding about 1 cup broth per batch.
7. Return puréed soup to pot along with apple juice and remaining broth.
8. Season with salt and pepper.
9. Serve hot, sprinkled with parsley or chives.

Yields: 8 servings.

Ham and Barley Soup

This is a delicious soup that is hearty and satisfying.
Serve it hot from the stove with homemade biscuits or bread.
Make extra because this is even better the second day.

Ingredients:

  8 lg. celery stalks
  8 lg. carrots
  2 med. onions, diced
  6 qt. water
  4 c. ham
  2½ c. barley
  32 oz. tomatoes, stewed or crushed
  18 oz. frozen Italian green beans
     salt and pepper to taste

Directions:

  1. Cut celery into ¼-inch slices; cut carrots into pieces.
  2. In large Dutch oven or soup pot over medium-high heat, place cut vegetables, 6 quarts water, ham, barley, salt, and pepper.
  3. Cover and simmer for 1½ hours.
  4. Skim any fat from soup.
  5. Add tomatoes and beans; heat to boiling.
  6. Cover and simmer on low 10 minutes.

Yields: 18 servings.

Did You Know? . . . .

Did you know that in 2005 the two turkeys pardoned by the President were named Marshmallow and Yam?

Roasted Squash Soup

This is another hearty fall soup.

Ingredients for soup:

1	butternut squash (2½ lb.)
1	c. chopped onion
1	Tbs. minced fresh sage (or 1 tsp. rubbed sage)
1	pinch ground allspice
2	Tbs. butter
4	c. chicken broth
1	sm. tart apple, peeled, chopped
1½	tsp. lemon or lime juice
	pepper to taste

Ingredients for topping:

⅓	c. sour cream
½	tsp. lemon or lime juice
¼	tsp. grated lemon or lime peel

Directions for soup:

1. Preheat oven to 400 degrees F.
2. Cut squash in half lengthwise; scoop out seeds.
3. Place squash cut side down in greased baking dish.
4. Bake uncovered for 50 to 60 minutes or until tender.
5. When cool enough to handle, scoop out squash.
6. Place squash in bowl and mash; set aside.
7. In large saucepan sauté onion, sage, and allspice in butter until tender.
8. Add broth and apple; bring to a boil.
9. Reduce heat; cover and simmer until apple is tender, about 8 minutes.
10. Add reserved squash; simmer 5 minutes longer.
11. Cool until lukewarm.
12. In food processor or blender, process soup in batches until smooth; return to pan.
13. Add lemon juice and pepper; heat through.

Directions for topping:

1. Combine topping ingredients.
2. Place dollop on each serving.

Yields: 6 servings.

Vegetarian Corn Chowder

My children love this vegetable chowder.

Ingredients:

1 c. butter, divided
1 sm. onion, diced
2 c. diced red potatoes
2 c. diced carrots
2 c. diced celery
3 cans creamed corn
4 cans whole kernel corn (or 8 ears fresh)
2 c. milk
2 c. half-and-half
1 tsp. parsley
1 Tbs. chives
1 tsp. onion salt
½ tsp. garlic powder
   salt and pepper to taste

Directions:

1. Sauté onion in ⅞ cup butter until transparent.
2. Add potatoes, carrots, and celery; sauté.
3. Stir in corn, milk, half-and-half, parsley, chives, and seasonings.
4. Slice remaining butter on top.
5. Simmer about 1 hour.
6. Cool, then reheat and serve.

Turkey and Stuffin' Soup

Here is a different way to use leftovers from your Thanksgiving meal.

Ingredients:

> 4-6 c. leftover stuffing
> 1   Tbs. extra-virgin olive oil
> 2   med. carrots, chopped (or up to 2 c. leftover baby carrots, chopped)
> 2   ribs celery, chopped
> 1   onion, chopped
> 1   bay leaf
> 2   qt. turkey stock (recipe page 287)
> 1½ lb. light and dark cooked turkey meat, diced
> 1   c. frozen peas (or leftover prepared peas)
>   salt and pepper
>   handful of flat-leaf parsley leaves, chopped

Directions:

1. Preheat oven to 350 degrees F.
2. Transfer stuffing into small baking dish.
3. Place dish in oven and reheat 12 to 15 minutes, until warmed through.
4. Meanwhile, heat olive oil in large pan over moderate heat.
5. Add carrots, celery, and onion; lightly season with salt and pepper.
6. Add bay leaf and stock; raise heat and bring to a boil.
7. Add turkey and reduce heat to simmer.
8. Simmer until any raw vegetables are tender, about 10 minutes.
9. Stir in parsley and peas.
10. Remove stuffing from oven.
11. Using ice cream scoop, place a healthy scoop of stuffing in center of soup bowl.
12. Ladle soup around stuffing ball and serve.

Yields: 2 quarts (4 to 6 servings).

Sweet Potato Kale Soup

White kidney beans, sweet potatoes, kale, and plenty of garlic flavor this brothy blend.

Ingredients:

- 4 oz. fresh kale
- 1 lg. onion, chopped
- 3½ tsp. Italian Seasoning (recipe page 177)
- 2 tsp. olive oil
- 3 cans vegetable broth (14½ oz. each)
- 2 cans white kidney or cannelloni beans (15-oz. each), rinsed, drained
- 1 lb. sweet potatoes, peeled, cubed
- 12 cloves garlic, minced
- ½ tsp. salt
- ¼ tsp. pepper

Directions:

1. Cut out and discard thick vein from each kale leaf; coarsely chop kale and set aside.
2. In large Dutch oven or soup kettle, sauté onion and Italian seasoning in oil until onion is tender.
3. Stir in broth, beans, sweet potatoes, and kale.
4. Bring to a boil.
5. Reduce heat; simmer uncovered for 10 minutes.
6. Stir in garlic, salt, and pepper.
7. Simmer 10 to 15 minutes longer or until potatoes are tender.

Yields: 8 servings.

***Did You Know?* . . . .**

Did you know that there is no evidence to support the claim that turkey was served at the first Thanksgiving?

Turkey Chili

Use fresh ground turkey for this delicious chili.

Ingredients:

1	lg. yellow onion, chopped
6	cloves garlic, minced
2	Tbs. cumin seed
6	Tbs. olive oil, divided
2	red bell peppers, chopped
2	poblano peppers, chopped
2	jalapenos, seeded, chopped
2	serrano chilies, seeded, chopped
1	c. ancho chili paste
3	Tbs. red chili powder
1	Tbs. ground coriander
1	Tbs. ground cinnamon
1	Tbs. black pepper
2	lb. ground turkey
4	c. tomatoes with juice, chopped
2	c. chicken stock
1	c. beer
7	oz. chipotle peppers in adobo sauce
¼	c. unsweetened chocolate, grated
	green onion, chopped
	cilantro
	cheese, grated
	tortilla strips, fired
	sour cream

Directions:

1. Sauté onion, garlic, and cumin seeds in 3 tablespoons olive oil in Dutch oven until onions are soft.
2. Stir in peppers; sauté for 10 minutes.

3. Add chili paste, chili powder, coriander, cinnamon, and pepper.
4. Sauté, stirring, 5 to 7 minutes.
5. In another skillet brown ground turkey in remaining 3 tablespoons olive oil.
6. Drain off any fat.
7. Combine pepper mixture, turkey, tomatoes, chicken stock, beer, and chipotle peppers in Dutch oven.
8. Simmer for 45 to 60 minutes.
9. Stir in chocolate and serve.
10. Garnish with green onions, cilantro, cheese, tortilla strips, and sour cream.

Yields: 8 servings.

Turkey Stock

My husband always makes turkey soup after any turkey dinner, so nothing is ever wasted.

Ingredients:

1 turkey carcass
2 stalks celery with leaves, coarsely chopped
2 carrots, coarsely chopped
1 onion, peeled, quartered
1 bay leaf
8 c. water

Directions:

1. In large pot combine all stock ingredients and bring to a simmer.
2. Simmer for 2 to 3 hours over medium-low heat.
3. Strain and discard vegetables and bones.
4. Reserve stock.

Turkey Green Chili

Poblano and jalapeno chilies, tomatillos, and cilantro account for this recipe's title.

Ingredients:

- 1½ lb. poblano chilies
- 2   Tbs. olive oil
- ½   lb. pork, chicken, or turkey chorizo sausages, casings removed
- 3   c. chopped onions
- 6   lg. cloves garlic, chopped
- 2   Tbs. chili powder
- 1   tsp. ground cumin
- 5   lb. turkey thighs with bones, skinned, boned, meat cut into 1-inch cubes
- 2   c. chicken broth
- 12 oz. fresh tomatillos, husked, rinsed, chopped
- 1   c. canned diced tomatoes, drained
- ½   c. chopped fresh cilantro stems
- 2   Tbs. or more fresh lime juice
- 1   Tbs. chopped jalapeno chili with seeds
     salt and pepper

Directions:

1. Char poblanos directly over gas flame or in broiler until blackened on all sides.
2. Enclose in plastic bag; let stand 10 minutes then peel, seed, and chop poblanos.
3. Heat oil in large pot over medium heat.
4. Add chorizo; sauté until cooked through, breaking up with back of fork, about 5 minutes.
5. Add onions and garlic.
6. Cover and cook 10 minutes.
7. Mix in chili powder and cumin.
8. Sprinkle turkey with salt and pepper; add to pot and stir.
9. Add broth and next 5 ingredients.
10. Mix in roasted poblanos.
11. Bring chili to a boil, stirring occasionally.

12. Reduce heat to medium-low, and simmer uncovered until turkey is tender, about 45 minutes.
13. Season chili with more lime juice, if desired, and salt and pepper.
14. Serve hot.
15. Chili can be made 2 days ahead.
16. Chill uncovered until cold, then cover and keep chilled.
17. Re-warm before serving.

Yields: 8 servings.

Harvest Sweet Potato Soup

This soup is thick and nutritious. It can be served warm or chilled.

Ingredients:

1 c. chopped celery
½ c. chopped onion
1 Tbs. vegetable oil
3 med. sweet potatoes (about 1 lb.), peeled, cubed
3 c. chicken broth
1 bay leaf
½ tsp. dried basil
 salt to taste

Directions:

1. In Dutch oven or soup kettle, sauté celery and onion in oil until tender.
2. Add remaining ingredients; bring to a boil over medium heat.
3. Reduce heat; simmer for 25 to 30 minutes or until tender.
4. Discard bay leaf.
5. Cool slightly.
6. In food processor or blender, process soup in batches until smooth.
7. Return all to pan and heat through.

Yields: 4 servings.

Turkey Stew with Dumplings

This mild-tasting, homey dish has flavorful dumplings floating on a tasty turkey and vegetable stew. It really hits the spot on chilly fall and winter days. Make extra dumplings because they will disappear quickly.

Ingredients for stew:

12   med. carrots, cut into 1-inch chunks
8   celery ribs, cut into 1-inch chunks
1   c. chopped onion
½   c. butter
4   cans chicken broth (10 oz. each) or 5 c. homemade turkey stock (recipe page 287)
3⅓ c. water, divided
2   tsp. salt
¼   tsp. pepper
3   c. cubed cooked turkey
2   c. frozen cut green beans
½   c. all-purpose flour
1   tsp. Worcestershire sauce

Ingredients for dumplings:

1½ c. all-purpose flour
2   tsp. baking powder
1   tsp. salt
2   Tbs. minced parsley
⅛   tsp. poultry seasoning (recipe page 178)
¾   c. milk
2   eggs

Directions for stew:

1. In Dutch oven or soup kettle, sauté carrots, celery, and onion in butter for 10 minutes.
2. Add broth, 3 cups water, salt, and pepper.
3. Cover and cook over low heat for 15 minutes or until vegetables are tender.
4. Add turkey and beans; cook for 5 minutes.
5. Combine flour, Worcestershire sauce, and remaining water until smooth; stir into turkey mixture.

6. Bring to a boil.
7. Reduce heat; cover and simmer for 5 minutes.

Directions for dumplings:

1. Combine flour, baking powder, and salt in bowl.
2. Stir in parsley and poultry seasoning.
3. Combine milk and egg; stir into flour mixture just until moistened.
4. Drop by tablespoonfuls onto simmering stew.
5. Cover and simmer for 10 minutes; uncover and simmer 10 minutes longer.

Yields: 10 to 12 servings.

Turkey Rice Soup

This is an easy-to-make, soothing soup.

Ingredients:

3   Tbs. butter
1   c. chopped onion
1   c. chopped celery
2   tsp. dried thyme
2   c. chopped carrots
1   c. rice
8   c. turkey stock (recipe page 287)
2   c. chopped leftover turkey
1   c. corn, frozen or leftover
3   Tbs. fresh parsley
    salt and pepper

Directions:

1. In large pot sauté onions in butter until tender.
2. Stir in celery and thyme.
3. Stir in carrots and rice; toss to coat.
4. Add turkey stock and bring to a simmer.
5. Cook until vegetables and rice are tender.
6. Stir in turkey, corn, and parsley.
7. Return to simmer, and season to taste with salt and pepper.

Clam and Corn Chowder

This recipe combines two favorite New England chowders in one. It is a family favorite. Serve it hot with crumbled crackers or soup crackers.

Ingredients:

- 8 slices bacon, coarsely chopped
- 1 med. onion, chopped
- 1 lb. russet potatoes, peeled, cubed
- ½ tsp. salt
- ¼ tsp. ground black pepper
- 4 cans chopped clams (6½ oz. each), drained, with juice reserved
- 1½ c. milk
- 1½ c. fresh or frozen corn kernels
- 1½ c. half-and-half
- 1 Tbs. chopped fresh parsley leaves
  saltine or soup crackers

Directions:

1. In 5-quart Dutch oven or heavy pan, cook bacon over medium heat until crisp and browned.
2. Using slotted spoon, transfer bacon to paper towel; drain.
3. Pour fat into small heatproof bowl.
4. Return 1 tablespoon fat to Dutch oven; discard or freeze remaining fat.
5. Add onion to fat; cook, stirring occasionally, until softened, 2 to 3 minutes.
6. Add 2 cups water to Dutch oven, stirring to loosen browned bits on bottom.
7. Add potatoes, salt, pepper, and reserved clam juice; stir and cover.
8. Bring to a boil over high heat; reduce heat to low and cook until potatoes are fork-tender, about 10 minutes.
9. Stir in milk; return to a boil.
10. Add corn and half-and-half and cook 5 minutes.
11. Add reserved clams, and cook just until clams are heated through; stir in parsley and reserved bacon.

Yields: 6 servings.

Thanksgiving Delights Cookbook

A Collection of Thanksgiving Recipes
Cookbook Delights Holiday Series Book 11

Wines and Spirits

Table of Contents

Did You Know? . . .

Did you know that one crew member and one passenger of the Mayflower died before they reached land?

About Cooking with Alcohol

Some recipes in this cookbook contain, among other ingredients, liquors. It is for the purpose of obtaining desired flavor and achieving culinary appreciation and not to be abused in any way. In cooking and baking, alcohol evaporates and only the flavor may be enjoyed. When mixed in cold, however, such as in desserts, caution must be exercised. These recipes are intended for people who may consume small amounts of alcohol in a responsible and safe manner.

I live in Washington State and we are proud of our wine production. Washington State is rapidly gaining prestige as a premier wine producer. Do enjoy the art of wine tasting and enjoy the completeness and uniqueness of each wine. It is an art to enjoy and savor in moderation.

If consumption of even small amounts of alcoholic ingredients presents a problem, in whatever form, please substitute coffee flavor syrups, found in coffee sections of supermarkets. For example, instead of Southern Comfort liqueur, substitute with Irish Cream or Amaretto Syrup.

Karen Jean Matsko Hood

Cranberry, Gingerly

This is a spicy spin on the Cosmo. Enjoy it for the holidays.

Ingredients:

¼ c. vodka
2 Tbs. ginger beer
1½ Tbs. thawed cranberry juice cocktail concentrate
1½ tsp. lemon juice
⅛ tsp. ground ginger
ice
slice of crystallized ginger for garnish

Directions:

1. Shake vodka, beer, juices, and ground ginger with ice in cocktail shaker.
2. Strain into martini glass.
3. Garnish with slice of crystallized ginger.

Yields: 1 serving.

Crème de Vie

This is a rich drink that is perfect for the holidays. You will enjoy this creamy dessert drink.

Ingredients:

1   c. water
1   c. sugar
6   egg yolks
1   can sweetened condensed milk (14 oz.)
1   c. rum
1   tsp. vanilla extract

Directions:

1. In saucepan combine water and sugar.
2. Bring to a boil and cook for 3 minutes.
3. Place egg yolks in blender and process on high speed.
4. Slowly pour in hot sugar water while blending. (Pouring too fast might curdle yolks.)
5. Add condensed milk, rum, and vanilla.
6. Blend until smooth
7. Chill in refrigerator.

Yields: 8 servings.

Cranberry Bog Cocktail

Serve this cranberry cocktail in fancy glasses, and enjoy the bubbly.

Ingredients:

    4   oz. champagne
    1   oz. cranberry juice
        whole cranberries for garnish
        mint leaves for garnish

Directions:

1. Combine champagne and cranberry juice in champagne flute.
2. Drop a few whole cranberries in glass and garnish with mint leaves.

Yields: 1 serving.

Red Sangria

Sangria makes an attractive holiday drink.

Ingredients:

    1   gal. Burgundy wine
    1   qt. orange juice
    1   c. lemon juice
    ½   c. sugar
    ½   c. brandy
    ¼   c. Cointreau
    1   qt. club soda, chilled
    2   oranges, thinly sliced
    1   lemon, thinly sliced
         ice ring

Directions:

1. Mix wine, orange juice, lemon juice, sugar, brandy, and Cointreau; chill.
2. Add chilled soda and pour into punch bowl over an ice ring.
3. Float orange and lemon slices on top.

Yields: 10 servings.

Cranberry Hot Toddies

Hot toddies sound so inviting. They add warmth to your holiday menu.

Ingredients:

4   tangerines
½   c. whole cloves
3   qt. pure, unsweetened cranberry juice (if unavailable, use cranberry juice cocktail and omit sugar)
2   c. sugar or to taste
3   c. amber rum

Directions:

1. Cut tangerines crosswise into ¼-inch-thick rounds; remove seeds.
2. Stud rind of each tangerine round with 4 or 5 cloves.
3. In large saucepan simmer cranberry juice, tangerine rounds, and sugar, covered, for 5 minutes.
4. Stir in rum.
5. Serve toddies with clove-studded tangerine rounds in heatproof glasses.

Apple Pie Drink

This is a very good fall weather drink. It is great either hot or cold.

Ingredients:

- 1 gal. apple juice
- 1 gal. apple cider
- 1 c. brown sugar, firmly packed
- 10 cinnamon sticks
- 1 bottle vodka (750 milliliters)

Directions:

1. In large pot combine apple juice, apple cider, sugar, and cinnamon sticks.
2. Bring to a boil; remove from heat and let cool completely.
3. When juice mixture is cool, stir in vodka.
4. Serve hot or cold.

Pumpkin Nog

A combination of pumpkin, evaporated milk, cinnamon, and ice cream makes up this scrumptious drink for your holiday meal.

Ingredients:

- 1 can pumpkin purée (15 oz.)
- 1 can evaporated milk (12 oz.)
- 2 Tbs. honey
- 1 tsp. ground cinnamon
- 1 pt. vanilla ice cream
- 3 Tbs. rum
    ground nutmeg

Directions:

1. Place pumpkin, milk, honey, and cinnamon in blender container; cover.
2. Blend until smooth.
3. Add ice cream and rum.
4. Blend until smooth.
5. Sprinkle with nutmeg; serve immediately.

Yields: 8 servings.

Hot Tea Toddy

A hot tea toddy is a nice variation for the tea lover.

Ingredients:

1   Irish breakfast tea bag
1½ oz. Scotch or brandy
1   Tbs. honey (heaping)
½   cinnamon stick
1   slice lemon
    boiling water
    pinch ground nutmeg

Directions:

1. In coffee mug place tea bag, Scotch, and honey.
2. Add enough boiling water (about ¾ cup) to fill mug.
3. Add cinnamon and lemon; steep for 5 minutes.
4. Remove tea bag and cinnamon stick.
5. Sprinkle lightly with nutmeg and serve.

Yields: 1 serving.

Apple Pie Shot

This is a mouth-watering vodka shot that tastes like mom's apple pie. Put the entire shot in your mouth and swish it back and forth a few times before swallowing.

Ingredients:

- 1 fl. oz. vodka
- 1 fl. oz. apple cider
- 1 Tbs. whipped cream
- 1 pinch ground cinnamon

Directions:

1. In 2-oz. shot glass, combine vodka and apple cider.
2. Top with dollop of whipped cream and a pinch of cinnamon.

Yields: 1 serving.

Fried Wild Turkey

This is a unique name for your holiday drink.

Ingredients:

- 1 can or bottle lemon-lime flavored soda (12 oz.)
- 1 jigger bourbon whiskey (1.5 oz.)
- 1 jigger hazelnut liqueur (1.5 oz.)
  ice

Directions:

1. Fill tall glass with ice.
2. Fill to ¾ full with lemon-lime soda.
3. Pour in bourbon whiskey and hazelnut liqueur.
4. Stir and serve.

Yields: 1 serving.

Eggnog

This is a delicious eggnog that can be made with or without alcohol.

Ingredients:

    3   c. whole milk
    7   lg. eggs
    1   c. sugar
    2   c. heavy cream
    1   tsp. vanilla extract
    ⅓   c. bourbon (optional)
    ⅓   c. Cognac or other brandy (optional)
        freshly grated nutmeg

Directions:

1. Bring milk just to a boil in 2-quart heavy saucepan.
2. Whisk together eggs and sugar in large bowl.
3. Add hot milk in slow stream, whisking.
4. Pour mixture into saucepan and cook over moderately low heat, stirring constantly with wooden spoon, until mixture registers 170 degrees on thermometer, 6 to 7 minutes.
5. Pour custard through fine-mesh sieve into clean large bowl and stir in cream and vanilla; add bourbon and brandy, if desired.
6. Cool completely, uncovered, then chill, covered, until cold, at least 3 hours and up to 24.
7. Serve sprinkled with freshly grated nutmeg.
8. Note: Flavor of eggnog improves when made a day ahead to allow alcohol to mellow.

Yields: About 6 cups.

Cranberry Mojitos

This is a festive Thanksgiving drink.

Ingredients:

 1　bunch fresh mint, trimmed (about 1 c.)
 ½　c. sugar
 1¾　c. light rum
 1¼　c. fresh lime juice
 1　can cranberry juice concentrate, reconstituted
 6　c. ice

Directions:

1. Using wooden spoon, mash mint with sugar in bottom of large pitcher.
2. Add rum and lime juice; stir to dissolve sugar.
3. Mix in thawed cranberry juice concentrate and water, according to directions on can; add to pitcher.
4. Mix in ice.

Yields: 6 servings.

Rock and Roll

Try this autumnal, herbaceous twist on the martini.

Ingredients:

 2　rosemary sprigs, divided
 1　thyme sprig
 1　dash dry vermouth
 　gin
 　ice
 　martini olive

Directions:

1. Muddle 1 rosemary sprig, thyme sprig, and a dash of dry vermouth in cocktail shaker.
2. Add ice and gin.
3. Shake; strain through fine sieve into martini glass.
4. Garnish with a green martini olive skewered on a rosemary sprig.

Yields: 1 serving.

Original Irish Cream

This recipe makes a great gift for your family and friends. It also makes a pleasant drink.

Ingredients:

1   c. heavy cream
1   can sweetened condensed milk (14 oz.)
1⅔ c. Irish whiskey
1   tsp. instant coffee granules
2   Tbs. chocolate syrup
1   tsp. vanilla extract
1   tsp. almond extract

Directions:

1. Combine all ingredients in blender; blend on high for 20 to 30 seconds.
2. Store in tightly sealed container in refrigerator.
3. Shake well before serving.
4. Will keep for 2 months if refrigerated.

Yields: 4 cups.

Hot Spiced Cider and Rum Punch

The spices and rum add great flavor to this punch.

Ingredients:

    3   sm. oranges, well washed, dried
    3   Tbs. whole cloves
    2   qt. apple cider
    2   cinnamon sticks (4-in. lengths)
    1½ c. light or dark rum

Directions:

1. Stud oranges with cloves; place in punch bowl.
2. Heat cider with cinnamon sticks in large saucepan.
3. Pour over oranges and add rum.
4. Serve warm in punch cups.

Yields: 12 servings.

Hot Spiked Cider

This is a "spiked" version of the traditional hot cider that is great for fall or holiday gatherings. It can be made in large quantities and kept warm in an electric coffee server.

Ingredients:

    1   qt. water
    3   orange spice tea bags
    ¼   c. light brown sugar, firmly packed
    2   c. apple cider
    1½ c. light rum
    8   cinnamon sticks, divided
    3   tsp. butter

Directions:

1. Pour water into large saucepan and bring to a boil.
2. Remove from heat and add orange spice tea bags.
3. Cover and let steep 5 minutes.
4. Remove tea bags and stir in sugar, apple cider, rum, and 2 cinnamon sticks.
5. Heat just to steaming. (Do not boil.)
6. Ladle hot cider into 6 mugs, and drop ½ teaspoon butter into each.
7. Garnish with cinnamon "swizzle" stick.

Yields: 6 servings.

Thanksgiving Turkey

This is another unique name for a holiday drink.

Ingredients:

1   jigger bourbon whiskey (1½ oz.)
½ c. orange juice
1   tsp. frozen lemonade concentrate
1   tsp. frozen limeade concentrate
⅓ c. ginger ale
    ice

Directions:

1. Fill tall glass with ice.
2. Pour in bourbon whiskey, orange juice, lemonade concentrate, and limeade concentrate.
3. Fill to top with ginger ale.
4. Stir and serve.

Yields: 1 serving.

Festival Information

Following is a list of just a few of the Thanksgiving festivals throughout the country each year.

Macy's Thanksgiving Day Parade
Thanksgiving Day
New York City, New York
www.macysparade.com
Moving stands with specific themes, scenes from Broadway plays, large balloons of cartoon characters and TV personalities, and high school marching bands.

New Orleans Athletic Club's "Turkey Day Race"
Thanksgiving Day
New Orleans, Louisiana
http://turkeydayrace.com
An annual historic 5-mile race benefiting local charities since 1986.

Turkey Beach Trot
Thanksgiving Day
Ocean Beach, San Francisco, California
www.turkeybeachtrot.com
8-mile race for adults, 3 miles for pilgrim promenade, and 100 meters for kids. "1620 Academy Award" goes to Best Leading Poultry, Best Supporting Male Pilgrim, Best Supporting Female Indian, Best Choreography, and Best Costumes.

Jeffersonian Thanksgiving Festival
Weekend before Thanksgiving and the day after
Charlottesville, Virginia
www.jeffersonthanksgiving.org or 434-249-4032
Over 60 events and activities designed to let you experience what this community was like during the American Revolution between 1779 and 1781.

U.S. and Metric Measurement Charts

Here are some measurement equivalents to help you with exchanges. There was a time when many people thought the entire world would convert to the metric scale. While most of the world has, America still has not. Metric conversions in cooking are vitally important to preparing a tasty recipe. Here are simple conversion tables that should come in handy.

U.S. Measurement Equivalents

A few grains/pinch/dash, (dry) = Less than ⅛ teaspoon
A dash (liquid) = A few drops
3 teaspoons = 1 tablespoon
½ tablespoon = 1½ teaspoons
1 tablespoon = 3 teaspoons
2 tablespoons = 1 fluid ounce
4 tablespoons = ¼ cup
5⅓ tablespoons = ⅓ cup
8 tablespoons = ½ cup
8 tablespoons = 4 fluid ounces
10⅔ tablespoons = ⅔ cup
12 tablespoons = ¾ cup
16 tablespoons = 1 cup
16 tablespoons = 8 fluid ounces
⅛ cup = 2 tablespoons
¼ cup = 4 tablespoons
¼ cup = 2 fluid ounces
⅓ cup = 5 tablespoons plus 1 teaspoon
½ cup = 8 tablespoons
1 cup = 16 tablespoons
1 cup = 8 fluid ounces
1 cup = ½ pint
2 cups = 1 pint
2 pints = 1 quart
4 quarts (liquid) = 1 gallon
8 quarts (dry) = 1 peck
4 pecks (dry) = 1 bushel
1 kilogram = approximately 2 pounds
1 liter = approximately 4 cups or 1 quart

Approximate Metric Equivalents by Volume

U.S.	Metric
¼ cup	= 60 milliliters
½ cup	= 120 milliliters
1 cup	= 230 milliliters
1¼ cups	= 300 milliliters
1½ cups	= 360 milliliters
2 cups	= 460 milliliters
2½ cups	= 600 milliliters
3 cups	= 700 milliliters
4 cups (1 quart)	= .95 liter
1.06 quarts	= 1 liter
4 quarts (1 gallon)	= 3.8 liters

Approximate Metric Equivalents by Weight

U.S.	Metric
¼ ounce	= 7 grams
½ ounce	= 14 grams
1 ounce	= 28 grams
1¼ ounces	= 35 grams
1½ ounces	= 40 grams
2½ ounces	= 70 grams
4 ounces	= 112 grams
5 ounces	= 140 grams
8 ounces	= 228 grams
10 ounces	= 280 grams
15 ounces	= 425 grams
16 ounces (1 pound)	= 454 grams

Glossary

Aerate: A synonym for sift; to pass ingredients through a fine-mesh device to break up large pieces and incorporate air into ingredients to make them lighter.

Al dente: "To the tooth," in Italian. The pasta is cooked just enough to maintain a firm, chewy texture.

Baste: To brush or spoon liquid fat or juices over meat during roasting to add flavor and prevent drying out.

Bias-slice: To slice a food crosswise at a 45-degree angle.

Bind: To thicken a sauce or hot liquid by stirring in ingredients such as eggs, flour, butter, or cream until it holds together.

Blanch: To scald, as in vegetables being prepared for freezing; as in almonds so as to remove skins.

Blend: To mix or fold two or more ingredients together to obtain equal distribution throughout the mixture.

Braise: To brown meat in oil or other fat and then cook slowly in liquid. The effect of braising is to tenderize the meat.

Bread: To coat food with crumbs (usually with soft or dry bread crumbs), sometimes seasoned.

Brown: To quickly sauté, broil, or grill either at the beginning or at the end of meal preparation, often to enhance flavor, texture, or eye appeal.

Brush: To use a pastry brush to coat a food such as meat or pastry with melted butter, glaze, or other liquid.

Butterfly: To cut open a food such as pork chops down the center without cutting all the way through, and then spread apart.

Caramelize: To brown sugar over a flame, with or without the addition of some water to aid the process. The temperature range in which sugar caramelizes is approximately 320 to 360 degrees F.

Char: To burn the surface of; scorch. Applies especially to chili peppers as a way to add flavor and remove the skin.

Chorizo: A highly seasoned, coarsely ground pork sausage that is widely used in Mexican and Spanish cooking.

Clarify: To remove impurities from butter or stock by heating the liquid, then straining or skimming it.

Coddle: A cooking method in which foods (such as eggs) are put in separate containers and placed in a pan of simmering water for slow, gentle cooking.

Comice Pear: A pear which originated in France, the Comice is the sweetest and juiciest of all varieties. It is a favorite in holiday boxes.

Confit: To slowly cook pieces of meat in their own gently rendered fat.

Core: To remove the inedible center of fruits such as pineapples.

Cream: To beat vegetable shortening, butter, or margarine, with or without sugar, until light and fluffy. This process traps in air bubbles, later used to create height in cookies and cakes.

Crimp: To create a decorative edge on a pie crust. On a double pie crust, this also seals the edges together.

Curd: A custard-like pie or tart filling flavored with juice and zest of citrus fruit, usually lemon, although lime and orange may also be used.

Curdle: To cause semisolid pieces of coagulated protein to develop in food, usually as a result of the addition of an acid substance, or the overheating of milk or egg-based sauces.

Custard: A mixture of beaten egg, milk, and possibly other ingredients such as sweet or savory flavorings, which are cooked with gentle heat, often in a water bath or double boiler. As pie filling, the custard is frequently cooked and chilled before being layered into a baked crust.

Deglaze: To add liquid to a pan in which foods have been fried or roasted, in order to dissolve the caramelized juices stuck to the bottom of the pan.

Dot: To sprinkle food with small bits of an ingredient such as butter to allow for even melting.

Dredge: To sprinkle lightly and evenly with sugar or flour. A dredger has holes pierced on the lid to sprinkle evenly.

Drippings: The liquids left in the bottom of a roasting or frying pan after meat is cooked. Drippings are generally used for gravies and sauces.

Drizzle: To pour a liquid such as a sweet glaze or melted butter in a slow, light trickle over food.

Dust: To sprinkle food lightly with spices, sugar, or flour for a light coating.

Egg Wash: A mixture of beaten eggs (yolks, whites, or whole eggs) with either milk or water. Used to coat cookies and other baked goods to give them a shine when baked.

Emulsion: A mixture of liquids, one being a fat or oil and the other being water based so that tiny globules of one are suspended in the other. This may involve the use of stabilizers, such as egg or custard. Emulsions may be temporary or permanent.

Entrée: A French term that originally referred to the first course of a meal, served after the soup and before the meat courses. In the United States, it refers to the main dish of a meal.

Fillet: To remove the bones from meat or fish for cooking.

Filter: To remove lumps, excess liquid, or impurities by passing through paper or cheesecloth.

Firm-Ball Stage: In candy making, the point where boiling syrup dropped in cold water forms a ball that is compact yet gives slightly to the touch.

Flambé: To ignite a sauce or other liquid so that it flames.

Flan: An open pie filled with sweet or savory ingredients; also, a Spanish dessert of baked custard covered with caramel.

Flute: To create a decorative scalloped or undulating edge on a pie crust or other pastry.

Fricassee: Usually a stew in which the meat is cut up, lightly cooked in butter, and then simmered in liquid until done.

Ganache: A rich chocolate filling or coating made with chocolate, vegetable shortening, and possibly heavy cream. It can coat cakes or cookies, and be used as a filling for truffles.

Glaze: A liquid that gives an item a shiny surface. Examples are fruit jams that have been heated or chocolate thinned with melted vegetable shortening. Also, to cover a food with such a liquid.

Hard-Ball Stage: In candy making, the point at which syrup has cooked long enough to form a solid ball in cold water.

Hull (also husk): To remove the leafy parts of soft fruits, such as strawberries or blackberries.

Infusion: To extract flavors by soaking them in liquid heated in a covered pan. The term also refers to the liquid resulting from this process.

Julienne: To cut into long, thin strips.

Jus: The natural juices released by roasting meats.

Marble: To gently swirl one food into another.

Marinate: To combine food with aromatic ingredients to add flavor.

Meringue: Egg whites beaten until they are stiff, then sweetened. It can be used as the topping for pies or baked as cookies.

Muddle: To mash or crush ingredients with a spoon or a muddler (a rod with a flattened end). Usually identified with the preparation of mixed drinks.

Mull: To slowly heat cider with spices and sugar.

Nonreactive Pan: Cookware that does not react chemically with foods, primarily acidic foods. Glass, stainless steel, enamel, anodized aluminum, and permanent nonstick surfaces are basically nonreactive. Shiny aluminum is reactive.

Parboil: To partly cook in a boiling liquid.

Peaks: The mounds made in a mixture. For example, egg white that has been whipped to stiffness. Peaks are "stiff" if they stay upright or "soft" if they curl over.

Pipe: To force a semisoft food through a bag (either a pastry bag or a plastic bag with one corner cut off) to decorate food.

Poblano: A mild, heart-shaped, dark green chili with very thick walls. When dried, poblanos are known as ancho chilies. They are the chili of choice for chilies rellenos.

Pressure Cooking: To cook using steam trapped under a locked lid to produce high temperatures and achieve fast cooking time.

Purée: To mash or sieve food into a thick liquid.

Ramekin: A small baking dish used for individual servings of sweet and savory dishes.

Reduce: To cook liquids down so that some of the water evaporates.

Roux: A cooked paste usually made from flour and butter used to thicken sauces.

Rugelach: A Jewish pastry with Polish origins, Rugelach means "little twists" in Yiddish. The dough is rolled around sweet filling such as chocolate, raisins and nuts, or preserves.

Sauté: To cook foods quickly in a small amount of oil in a skillet or sauté pan over direct heat.

Scald: To heat a liquid, usually a dairy product, until it almost boils.

Sear: To seal in a meat's juices by cooking it quickly using very high heat.

Seckel Pear: The smallest and sweetest of all commercially grown pears. Not much larger than bite-size, these sweet pears are sometimes called "sugar pears."

Sift: To remove large lumps from a dry ingredient such as flour or confectioners' sugar by passing it through a fine mesh. This process also incorporates air into the ingredients, making them lighter.

Simmer: To cook food in a liquid at a low enough temperature that small bubbles begin to break the surface.

Steam: To cook over boiling water in a covered pan. This method keeps foods' shape, texture, and nutritional value intact better than methods such as boiling.

Steep: To soak dry ingredients (tea leaves, ground coffee, herbs, spices, etc.) in liquid until the flavor is infused into the liquid.

Stewing: To brown small pieces of meat, poultry, or fish, then simmer them with vegetables or other ingredients in enough liquid to cover them, usually in a closed pot on the stove, in the oven, or with a slow cooker.

Thin: To reduce a mixture's thickness with the addition of more liquid.

Tomatillo: This fruit resembles a small green tomato except for its thin, papery husk and belongs to the same nightshade family as the tomato. Tomatillos are popular in Mexican and Southwest cooking.

Truss: To use string, skewers, or pins to hold together a food to maintain its shape while it cooks (usually applied to meat or poultry).

Vinaigrette: A general term referring to any sauce made with vinegar, oil, and seasonings.

Zest: The thin, brightly colored outer part of the rind of citrus fruits. It contains volatile oils, used as a flavoring.

Recipe Index of Thanksgiving Delights

314

315

Reader Feedback Form

Dear Reader,

We are very interested in what our readers think. Please fill in the form below and return it to:

Whispering Pine Press International, Inc.
c/o Thanksgiving Delights Cookbook
P.O. Box 214, Spokane Valley, WA 99037-0214
Phone: (509) 928-8700 | Fax: (509) 922-9949
Email: sales@whisperingpinepress.com
Publisher Websites: www.WhisperingPinePress.com
www.WhisperingPinePressBookstore.com
Blog: www.WhisperingPinePressBlog.com

Name: _____

Address: _____

City, St., Zip: _____

Phone/Fax: (____) _____ / (____) _____

Email: _____

Comments/Suggestions: _____

_____

_____

_____

A great deal of care and attention has been exercised in the creation of this book. Designing a great cookbook that is original, fun, and easy to use has been a job that required many hours of diligence, creativity, and research. Although we strive to make this book completely error free, errors and discrepancies may not be completely excluded. If you come across any errors or discrepancies, please make a note of them and send them to our publishing office. We are constantly updating our manuscripts, eliminating errors, and improving quality.

Please contact us at the address above.

About the Cookbook Delights Series

The *Cookbook Delights Series* includes many different topics and themes. If you have a passion for food and wish to know more information about different foods, then this series of cookbooks will be beneficial to you. Each book features a different type of food, such as avocados, strawberries, huckleberries, salmon, vegetarian, lentils, almonds, cherries, coconuts, lemons, and many, many more.

The *Cookbook Delights Series* not only includes cookbooks about individual foods but also includes several holiday-themed cookbooks. Whatever your favorite holiday may be, chances are we have a cookbook with recipes designed with that holiday in mind. Some examples include *Halloween Delights, Thanksgiving Delights, Christmas Delights, Valentine Delights, Mother's Day Delights, St. Patrick's Day Delights,* and *Easter Delights.*

Each cookbook is designed for easy use and is organized into alphabetical sections. Over 250 recipes are included along with other interesting facts, folklore, and history of the featured food or theme. Each book comes with a beautiful full-color cover, ordering information, and a list of other upcoming books in the series.

Note cards, bookmarks, and a daily journal have been printed and are available to go along with each cookbook. You may view the entire line of cookbooks, journals, cards, posters, puzzles, and bookmarks by visiting our website at www. thanksgivingdelights.com, or you can email us with questions and comments to: sales@whisperingpinepress.com.

Please ask your local bookstore to carry these sets of books.

To order, please contact:

Whispering Pine Press International, Inc.
c/o Thanksgiving Delights Cookbook
P.O. Box 214, Spokane Valley, WA 99037-0214
Phone: (509) 928-8700 | Fax: (509) 922-9949
Email: sales@whisperingpinepress.com
Publisher Websites: www.WhisperingPinePress.com
www.WhisperingPinePressBookstore.com
Blog: www.WhisperingPinePressBlog.com
SAN 253-200X

We Invite You to Join the
Whispering Pine Press International, Inc.,
Book Club!

Whispering Pine Press International, Inc.
c/o Thanksgiving Delights Cookbook
P.O. Box 214, Spokane Valley, WA 99037-0214
Phone: (509) 928-8700 | Fax: (509) 922-9949
Email: sales@whisperingpinepress.com
Publisher Websites: www.WhisperingPinePress.com
www.WhisperingPinePressBookstore.com
Blog: www.WhisperingPinePressBlog.com

Buy 11 books and get the next one free, based on the average price of the first eleven purchased.

How the club works:

Simply use the order form below and order books from our catalog. You can buy just one at a time or all eleven at once. After the first eleven books are purchased, the next one is free. Please add shipping and handling as listed on this form. There are no purchase requirements at any time during your membership. Free book credit is based on the average price of the first eleven books purchased.

Join today! Pick your books and mail in the form today!

Yes! I want to join the Whispering Pine Press International, Inc., Book Club! Enroll me and send the books indicated below.

Title   **Price**

1. _____
2. _____
3. _____
4. _____
5. _____
6. _____
7. _____
8. _____
9. _____
10. _____
11. _____

Free Book Title: _____

Free Book Price: _____ Avg. Price: _____ Total Price: _____

Credit for the free book is based on the average price of the first 11 books purchased.

(Circle one) Check | Visa | MasterCard | Discover | American Express

Credit Card #: _____ Expiration Date: _____

Name: _____

Address: _____

City: _____ State: _____ Country: _____

Zip/Postal: _____ Phone: (_____) _____

Email: _____

Signature_____

Whispering Pine Press International, Inc.
Fundraising Opportunities

Fundraising cookbooks are proven moneymakers and great keepsake providers for your group. Whispering Pine Press International, Inc., offers a very special personalized cookbook fundraising program that encourages success to organizations all across the USA.

Our prices are competitive and fair. Currently, we offer a special of 100 books with many free features and excellent customer service. Any purchase you make is guaranteed first-rate.

Flexibility is not a problem. If you have special needs, we guarantee our cooperation in meeting each of them. Our goal is to create a cookbook that goes beyond your expectations. We have the confidence and a record that promises continual success.

Another great fundraising program is the *Cookbook Delights Series* Program. With cookbook orders of 50 copies or more, your organization receives a huge discount, making for a prompt and lucrative solution.

We also specialize in assisting group fundraising–Christian, community, nonprofit, and academic among them. If you are struggling for a new idea, something that will enhance your success and broaden your appeal, Whispering Pine Press International, Inc., can help.

For more information, write, phone, or fax to:

Whispering Pine Press International, Inc.
P.O. Box 214
Spokane Valley, WA 99037-0214
Phone: (509) 928-8700 | Fax: (509) 922-9949
Email: sales@whisperingpinepress.com
Publisher Websites: www.WhisperingPinePress.com
www.WhisperingPinePressBookstore.com
Blog: www.WhisperingPinePressBlog.com
Book Website: www.ThanksgivingDelights.com
SAN 253-200X

Personalized and/or Translated Order Form for Any Book by Whispering Pine Press International, Inc.

Dear Readers:

If you or your organization wishes to have this book or any other of our books personalized, we will gladly accommodate your needs. For instance, if you would like to change the names of the characters in a book to the names of the children in your family or Sunday school class, we would be happy to work with you on such a project. We can add more information of your choosing and customize this book especially for your family, group, or organization.

We are also offering an option of translating your book into another language. Please fill out the form below telling us exactly how you would like us to personalize your book.

Please send your request to:

Whispering Pine Press International, Inc.
c/o Thanksgiving Delights Cookbook
P.O. Box 214, Spokane Valley, WA 99037-0214
Phone: (509) 928-8700 | Fax: (509) 922-9949
Email: sales@whisperingpinepress.com
Publisher Websites: www.WhisperingPinePress.com
www.WhisperingPinePressBookstore.com
Blog: www.WhisperingPinePressBlog.com

Person/Organization placing request: _____

Date_____ Phone: (____) _____

Address_____ Fax: (____) _____

City_____ State_____ Zip: _____

Language of the book: _____

Please explain your request in detail: _____

_____

_____

_____

_____

_____

_____

Thanksgiving Delights Cookbook

A Collection of Thanksgiving Recipes

How to Order

Get your additional copies of this book by returning an order form and your check, money order, or credit card information to:

Whispering Pine Press International, Inc.
c/o Thanksgiving Delights Cookbook
P.O. Box 214, Spokane Valley, WA 99037-0214
Phone: (509) 928-8700 | Fax: (509) 922-9949
Email: sales@whisperingpinepress.com
Publisher Websites: www.WhisperingPinePress.com
www.WhisperingPinePressBookstore.com
Blog: www.WhisperingPinePressBlog.com

Customer Name: _____

Address: _____

City, St., Zip: _____

Phone/Fax: _____

Email: _____

- -

Please send me _____ copies of _____
_____ at $_____ per copy and $4.95 for shipping and handling per book, plus $2.95 each for additional books. Enclosed is my check, money order, or charge my account for $_____.

☐ Check   ☐ Money Order   ☐ Credit Card

(*Circle One*) MasterCard | Discover | Visa | American Express

☐☐☐☐   ☐☐☐☐   ☐☐☐☐   ☐☐☐☐

Expiration Date: _____

_____
Signature

_____
Print Name

Whispering Pine Press International, Inc.
Your Northwest Book Publishing Company
P.O. Box 214
Spokane Valley, WA 99037-0214 USA
Phone: (509) 928-8700 | Fax: (509) 922-9949
Email: sales@whisperingpinepress.com
Publisher Websites: www.WhisperingPinePress.com
www.WhisperingPinePressBookstore.com

Shop Online:
www.whisperingpinepressbookstore.com
Fax orders to: (509)922-9949

Gift-wrapping, Autographing, and Inscription
We are proud to offer personal autographing by the author. For a limited time this service is absolutely free!
Gift-wrapping is also available for $4.95 per item.

1. Sold To

Name: _____
Street/Route: _____
_____
City: _____
State: _____ Zip: _____
Country: _____
Gift message: _____
_____
Email address: _____
Daytime Phone: (___) ___-____
*Necessary for verifying orders
Home Phone: (___) ___-____
Fax: (___) ___-____

2. Ship To

☐ Is this a new or corrected address?
☐ Alternative Shipping Address
☐ Mailing Address

Name: _____
Address: _____
_____
City: _____
State: _____ Zip: _____
Country: _____
Email address: _____

3. Items Ordered

ISBN # /Item #	Size	Color	Qty.	Title or Description	Price	Total

4. Method Of Payment

☐ Visa ☐ MasterCard ☐ Discover ☐ American Express
☐ Check/Money Order Please make it payable to Whispering Pine Press International, Inc. (No Cash or COD's)

Expiration Date
_____ / _____
Month   Year

Account Number

☐☐☐☐ ☐☐☐☐ ☐☐☐☐ ☐☐☐☐

Signature _____
Cardholder's signature
Printed Name _____
Please print name of cardholder
Address of Cardholder _____
_____

5. Shipping & Handling

Continental US
US Postal Ground: For books please add $4.95 for the first book and $2.95 each for additional books. All non-book items, add 15% of the Subtotal. Please allow 1-4 weeks for delivery.
US Postal Air: Please add $15.00 shipping and handling. Please allow 1-3 days for delivery

Alaska, Hawaii, and the US Territories
By Ship: Please add 10% shipping and handling (minimum charge $15.00). Please allow 6-12 weeks for delivery.
By Air: Please add 12% shipping and handling (minimum charge $15.00). Please allow 2-6 weeks for delivery.

International
By Ship: Please add 10% shipping and handling (minimum charge $15.00). Please allow 6-12 weeks for delivery.
By Air: Please add 12% shipping and handling (minimum charge $15.00). Please allow 2-6 weeks for delivery.
FedEx Shipments: Add $5.00 to the above airmail charges for overnight delivery.

Subtotal	
Gift wrap $4.95 Each	
For delivery in WA add 8.7% sales tax.	
Shipping See chart at left	
6. Total	

322

About the Author and Cook

Karen Jean Matsko Hood has always enjoyed cooking, baking, and experimenting with recipes. At this time Hood is working to complete a series of cookbooks that blends her skills and experience in cooking and entertaining. Hood entertains large groups of people and especially enjoys designing creative menus with holiday, international, ethnic, and regional themes.

Hood is publishing a cookbook series entitled the *Cookbook Delights Series*, in which each cookbook emphasizes a different food ingredient or theme. The first cookbook in the series is *Apple Delights Cookbook*. Hood is working to complete another series of cookbooks titled *Hood and Matsko Family Cookbooks*, which includes many recipes handed down from her family heritage and others that have emerged from more current family traditions. She has been invited to speak on talk radio shows on various topics, and favorite recipes from her cookbooks have been prepared on local television programs.

Hood was born and raised in Great Falls, Montana. As an undergraduate, she attended the College of St. Benedict in St. Joseph, Minnesota, and St. John's University in Collegeville, Minnesota. She attended the University of Great Falls in Great Falls, Montana. Hood received a B.S. Degree in Natural Science from the College of St. Benedict and minored in both Psychology and Secondary Education. Upon her graduation, Hood and her husband taught science and math on the island of St. Croix in the U.S. Virgin Islands. Hood has completed postgraduate classes at the University of Iowa in Iowa City, Iowa. In May 2001, she completed her Master's Degree in Pastoral Ministry at Gonzaga University in Spokane, Washington. She has taken postgraduate classes at Lewis and Clark College on the North Idaho college campus in Coeur d'Alene, Idaho, and Taylor University in Fort Wayne, Indiana. Hood is working on research projects to complete her Ph.D. in Leadership Studies at Gonzaga University in Spokane, Washington.

Hood resides in Greenacres, Washington, along with her husband, many of her sixteen children, and foster children. Her interests include writing, research, and teaching. She previously has volunteered as a court advocate in the Spokane juvenile court system for abused and neglected children. Hood is a literary advocate for youth and adults. Her hobbies include cooking, baking, collecting, photography, indoor and outdoor gardening, farming, and the cultivation of unusual flowering plants and orchids. She enjoys raising several specialty breeds of animals including Babydoll Southdown, Friesen, and Icelandic sheep, Icelandic horses, bichons frisés, cockapoos, Icelandic sheepdogs, a Newfoundland, a Rottweiler, a variety of Nubian and fainting goats, and a few rescue cats. Hood also enjoys bird-watching and finds all aspects of nature precious.

She demonstrates a passionate appreciation of the environment and a respect for all life. She also invites you to visit her websites:

www.KarenJeanMatskoHood.com
www.KarenJeanMatskoHoodBookstore.com
www.KarenJeanMatskoHoodBlog.com
www.KarensKidsBooks.com
www.KarensTeenBooks.com

www.HoodFamilyBlog.com
www.HoodFamily.com

Author's Social Media
Friend her on **Facebook:** Karen Jean Matsko Hood Author Fan Page
Please Follow the Author on **Twitter:** @KarenJeanHood
Google Plus Profile: Karen Jean Matsko Hood
Pinterest.com/KarenJMHood

CPSIA information can be obtained at www.ICGtesting.com
Printed in the USA
BVOW07*0751111114

373818BV00001B/1/P

9 781594 341649